MOSTLY
TAILFEATHERS

MOSTLY TAILFEATHERS

*Stories About Guns and Dogs
and Birds and Other
Odds and Ends*

GENE HILL

Drawings by Gordon M. Allen, Jr.

WINCHESTER
PRESS

Reprinted from Sports Afield Magazine
Text copyright © 1971, 1972, 1973 and 1974 by The Hearst Corporation
Illustrations copyright © 1975 by Gordon M. Allen, Jr.
All rights reserved

Library of Congress Catalog Card Number: 74-16873
ISBN: 0-87691-167-X (regular edition)
ISBN: 0-87691-171-8 (limited edition)

Published by Winchester Press
460 Park Avenue, New York 10022

Printed in the United States of America

To my mother and father
and for Lamar Underwood—
a good man to walk along life's rivers with

FOREWORD

THE LIFE of a writer is supposed to be lonely and stark. Mine has been anything but. I have been most privileged to have shared my pleasures with many singular people. I have enjoyed their constant encouragement and wisdom, their wit and humor.

Whatever I am I owe in no small part to Jim Rikhoff, Ed Zern, Dick Wolters, Harry Tennison, George Coe, Joe Hudson, Drew Holl, George Schielke—my thanks to you for being a very special part of my life.

And to Mac Dunn, Ralf Coykendall, Larry Koller, Dick and John Alden Knight, Milt Weiler—who still travel with me—my thanks to you for showing me how a gentleman should hunt and fish.

CONTENTS

BEING THERE

IT'S ONLY FAIR that you ask, "Who is Gene Hill?" I will attempt to answer that very fair question without undue modesty or puffery.

I am here writing odds and ends about this and that, and obviously I hope you enjoy them. But to start to really answer your question let me tell you that I am that other voice of the outdoors—the nonexpert. The things I can brag about are by all standards small potatoes indeed. For example, I like to shoot skeet and trap, and occasionally when the gathering is small, the air is still, and the good shots are off somewhere else with their peers I will add to my small collection of third and fourth places. I also like to train my own bird dogs—a collection of animals that are a far cry from the legendary "gentleman's shooting dog." Not much there to brag about either, in all honesty, except that we sort of complement each other. I am fond of them in the extreme and they are tolerant of my shortcomings—which is all, in fairness, that I can ask.

Nobody likes to think of himself as "average" when it comes to his outdoor skills, but there are too many times when I've been tested, and proved wanting, to classify myself as anything else. If, however, a category was just set aside for dreamers, I guess I could hold my own with just about anybody.

If I have a reason for being, it's contained in my small-boy curiosity and wonder. The tunneling of the mole is as intriguing in its small way as an earthquake; the long-drawn notes of a single goose are as mysterious to my ear as the stars are to my eyes.

In a duckblind I'm as eager and hopeful in the last lingering minutes of shooting as I am before dawn. I can get up and get out on any tomorrow believing wholeheartedly that today will be the day I get my double on woodcock in spite of the fact that yesterday I missed four easy straightaways in a row. I don't mind getting wet, lost or skunked. I don't mind being there now—when I should've been there yesterday or last week. I don't even care if you get all the easy shots and mine are all screamers; I've come to expect that sort of thing.

I just like being there—wet, cold or a little bit lost. I'm there, like you, to listen to the promises on the wind. To watch the soaring of the hawk, to catch the evening call "bobwhite, bobwhite," to see a sunset that I've never seen before or to have the day unfold and offer some small adventure that I've never had.

I just like being there, in my waterproof boots that leak, wearing my briarproof britches that cover my scratched and torn-up shanks. When you ask me how I've done, I'm always between telling you that I haven't seen anything, which might make me out to be an unobservant cuss, or admitting I've had a couple shots and missed.

BEING THERE

I just like being there because I love shotguns and bird dogs (yours—as much as, or more than, mine). I like the heft of half a box of shells in each pocket of my coat, and the security of having a pocketknife and "emergency stuff" such as a piece of rope and some waterproof matches that I'll never use. I like a dog that can catch parts of my sandwiches in midair until he ends up having most of my lunch. I like carrying duck calls and goose calls—but I never use one unless I'm miles from another blind. I like big red handkerchiefs and soft felt hats and hip boots with patches on them. I like the smell of wet dogs, northeast winds, woodcock swamps, gun oil, bourbon whiskey, pipesmoke and roasting ducks. I hope I'll always have a puppy to play with, a gun to trade and a new bird cover to try out. If you learn anything here at all it'll be about little things: a recipe, or a new book or an old favorite story. If I represent anything at all it will be the voices of the owls from black velvet skies, the bossy little bark of the fox, the following of tracks in a fresh skiff of snow from nowhere to nowhere. We'll talk about "why" instead of "how," with our stocking feet up on the good furniture and the dogs curled up in front of the fire. We'll talk about *being there*. That's why I'm here.

THE FUMBLERS

THERE'S A PRETTY funny joke we all know that ends with the line "everybody got to be someplace!"

As much as I agree with that homely truism, I am forced to roll my eyes upward and ask The Man Who Lives Upstairs "Why does it always have to be me?" I don't mean to complain, but it must be more than coincidence that the guy on the stand not a hundred yards from mine always gets his buck. The blind just across the little bay from where I shiver through the early-morning flights always take their limits before breakfast leaving me there to crunch a withered and sere sandwich and sip the dregs of cold coffee long past noon, at which time I finally give it up.

Given any hedgerow in a full section of beanfields, you'll get the two with the big coveys of quail, and I'll get the ones left where the red-winged blackbirds live.

Let me choose the fields where the mourning doves will flock to feed, and you take what's left over, and I'll have to come over to your house for dove dinner.

Guess who gets the pheasant shots when I'm stationed at the end of the cornfield drive? Why, the drivers, that's who.

If there's a secret about being the right guy in the right place at the right time, I haven't been able to break the code. In a river full of smallmouths, however, guess who caught the most fish out of the best looking white water? Me. But they weren't smallmouths—chubs, brother, chubs—and one on every cast.

I worked over a beautiful 15-pound salmon last summer and was down to one last fly in my book to try when a friend waded over, cast the identical fly I'd been going to try next—and that's how I know the salmon weighed 15 pounds.

When the guy I'm with says "Let me take just one more cast," or "I just want to spend another minute working out this cover," this guy, me, will end up saying, with a forced smile and a forked tongue, "Gee, that's the best fish I've seen here all summer," or "Gee, that's a beautiful double on woodcock—that's the first nice flight I've seen here all fall."

The philosophers tell us that there is an order in the nature of things, a "rightness," a logic—even if it isn't always apparent to us. It is not ours to question, but to meekly wait our turn. They tell us it will all equal out in the end, but I'm not so sure right now. If it does, I'm going to have some hot days coming.

But we all know that there are at least two kinds of hot days. Yours and the other fellow's, mainly. Yours is the day you are surrounded by birds right out of the car, and you've got that new 20-gauge you saved all year to buy. Oh, boy! Except you have two pockets full of 12-gauge shells, and the other guy is shooting 16s. I had a hot day last year. Lord knows how many miles from the camp in a duckblind with an automatic that I'd carefully cleaned—but forgot to put the rings back in. That was almost as

hot as the day I watched a big muley buck walk down a moun-
tainside toward me and discovered that my scope was filled with
snow; the other fellow got him. And the other fellow got my
geese.

There's always the "other fellow." His waders never leak.
He never forgets the rings in his automatic duck gun. He never
has the wrong shells, the wild bird dog or the sun constantly in
his eyes. The trap never breaks down just when he's run 20
straight, and his wife never shrinks his old hunting pants.

The cook never forgets to put three sugars in his coffee
thermos and he never loses his hunting license. He can get three-
minute eggs in an all-night diner, and the machine is never out of
his brand of cigarettes. He's the guy our wives should have married. He doesn't need glasses or dentists, and never loses his rain-
coat or drinks too much. And he's always around to be measured
against. Often enough, there's two of him. He never forgets,
when he's packing for a trip and it's hot and sunny at home, that
it's going to be cold and rainy where he's going. And he's never
our size so we can't borrow from him.

The ideal hunting/fishing companion would be overweight,
mindful of good bourbon, carry three gauges of shells in various
shot sizes, pack two of everything and like three sugars in his
thermos.

He should be an indifferent shot with a first-rate dog that
minds, and a poor caster who prefers to row the boat. He should
be a good cook who also likes to wash and dry dishes and ties super flies and gives them away. He ought to know how to tie nail
knots, do simple gun repair and carry boot patches as a matter of
course. And just one more little thing—dance with our wives at
the gun-club dinners while we stand around the bar and tell
stories.

I could add a few more details, but that would be greedy—
and I'd end up with a guy that wouldn't have anything to do with

the likes of us in the first place. Anyway, he'd make us uncomfortable.

Some of my friends manage, by mistake or accident, to descend to my level—every once in a while. But never when there's anybody else around. If I manage to ham-hand a nice fish and lose it when it's right up to the boat, there's always somebody around with it all on a movie camera; in perfect focus.

If I have a lousy round at trap, it's the day I invite the one guy I took the liberty of bragging to about how I almost won the club championship. And the good Lord forbid I ever brag up one of my dogs before a hunt!

I used to play a little baseball, and we had a right-fielder aptly named "Fumbler" Dowling. But Fumbler always brought beer . . . and played next to a center-fielder who was capable of playing the whole outfield all by himself.

But where are the Fumblers of our youth now that we need them? Why can't the guy who never breaks more than 18 be in our squad? Why is it that no one ever pushes deer our way? Where's the buddy with the massive backlash just as the bass begin feeding? There must be somebody else in the world who forgets the rings in his automatic, or Remington wouldn't carry them in their parts catalog.

The "other" guy is the same fellow who can wear a shirt marked LARGE and not find the collar too tight and the sleeves too long. He never gets bills marked "postage due," and factory trap stocks were made precisely to his measurements. His waders come up that crucial inch higher than mine, and his bunkmate never snores. All the "other" guys I fish and hunt with know how to do the double-haul and can lead crossing mallard downwind in a gale.

But when you stop to think about it, where would the "other" guys be without the likes of us? They wouldn't stand out the way they do now. Wives wouldn't have anything to complain about (?), and our children wouldn't cover us with the Sunday paper when their friends come to call.

Come to think of it—I guess they all tolerate us because we make everybody else look good.

I used to be a bit bothered by my inability to be "smooth," but not only have I learned to live with it, so have a few others around me. Not long ago I came home from a shoot at the gun club that I'd sworn I would win. When my daughter asked me how I'd done, I admitted that I was a mess. "That's all right, Daddy," she said, "you're *our* mess."

ACTING RICH

SOONER OR LATER most of us discover that there are, unfortu-
nately, no great aunts or uncles who are determined to name us
their favorite relative. We also know too well that daily labor at
our appointed tasks hardly keeps us even, and we have only the
magic of the Irish Sweepstakes or the like to come and pluck us
from our struggle in financial quicksand and swoop us to the
heady peaks of affluence.

I am always horribly disappointed to read in the paper about
some guy who hits the big one and is photographed holding a
check that represents $50,000 a year for life. He is more than
likely to say, "I don't think this will change our way of life too
much. Barbara and I will put the money in the bank and I guess
I'll just stay on doing what I'm doing." Well, you can bet your
leather-topped rubbers that it would sure change my life! I am

9

not in the habit of banking money and I do not intend to start now. And as for continuing to work every day, an attitude like that could give the whole gambling thing a bad name.

But should this be the year that The Telegram arrives from Dublin, are you ready? Have you been practicing that different tone of voice that wealth entitles you to? Will you ever send back an overdone sirloin to the chef? Have you ever refused to tip a nasty, inefficient waiter? Why not start now?

Take, for example, the following letter. Save it if you like. It can be used as a form to follow for tone of voice, attitude, etc. I have, of course, written others in order to have them ready—to my gunmakers, my plantation overseer and my private pilot. But this will do to start off.

Messrs. _____ , Tailors
00 Savile Row, London, England
My Dear Sirs:
The three shooting suits ordered on the 16th inst. have arrived— quite tardily as usual. Your constant refusal to use more than a few pennies for postage has ensured that the package has journeyed to the United States via Tasmania, Borneo and Guam. At the prices you are charging me I was led to expect hand delivery via Royal Messenger. My disappointment at the condition of the garments is only matched by my complete disbelief that you actually measured me when I was in London following my last shoot at my estate in Scotland.

It is of course remotely possible that you do have another customer named Gene Hill who is apparently in the employ of a European circus as the lead dwarf. The tightness of the sleeves in the dun-colored, unfinished worsted could lead to severe circulatory problems were it not for the fact that the breadth across the shoulders is so scant that it is impossible for me to wear the jacket more than five minutes at a time without requiring assistance from my valet in disrobing.

The beige covert-cloth model with the Campbell tartan lining is a comparable masterpiece. I was actually able to put it on without assistance and was very nearly able to button the front.

I immediately took up my favorite Churchill (the one with the 25-inch barrels I mentioned to you) and swung as if at a crossing bird. The resultant ripping sound so startled my man Baldwin that he nearly let the Purdey I was preparing to try next drop from his gloved hands. I was fully prepared to shred the garment in anger but you had foreseen that, I'm sure, by so constructing it that it fell apart, panel by panel, before I could do any real violence to the material.

As for the shepherd's check of which I was so especially fond, I have given it to Baldwin, who, you may recall, is constructed along the lines of a Bartlett pear and who carries himself with a curious stooping list, most of which is due to a legendary affection for the grape. However, the poor wretch is pleased with the garment as it fits him perfectly. I have deducted half of its cost from his wages and he talks constantly of my generosity. I do not expect you to try to extort payment from me for the other half if you value our long relationship. Along with the two suits I am returning you will find a blue denim jacket that I am enclosing for size; please return this with the two suits as I still occasionally shoot quail with my relatives.

I am most pleased with the neckties, both in fit and cut. I'm sure that the only reason we don't have them that narrow over here is that the bootlace companies would object to unfair competition.

My solicitors in London, Navin & Openshaw, assure me that my case against you for misrepresentation will be eagerly received in your courts should I not be in receipt of the above garments within 90 days.

Most cordially,
GENE HILL

11

THINGS HOMEMADE

THE SIMPLE WORD "homemade" is as honest as the work it describes. It separates and defines something special from the everyday. Like homemade bread—or homemade jam; homemade things are something someone loved doing.

Christmas past (because I'd been very good all year, I suppose), I was given a homemade trout net. And it's an object of more than ordinary beauty. A little uneven here and there, compared to store-bought nets, but it fits my uneven hand. It has a balance that could only have been created by someone feeling his way through the wood to make it come alive. It's art, and caring and knowing how are what art really is.

Too few things we have today are still homemade—like the wooden plugs an old friend once carved for me and the hammered brass wobblers a blacksmith gave me every spring to fish for pickerel in the ponds. I know a lot of things that are today still made by hands—but homemade, to me, means made by one person, not a group of people who assemble parts they've made into a single piece.

One of the reasons I like homemade things so much is that I'm so completely unable to make anything myself. Thoroughly awed by the carver's touch, ignorant of the art of the file, I stand in awe of anyone who can produce anything barely this side of shoddy.

So I eagerly collect the handmade things that come my way. A duck call, a half-dozen or so decoys, a few bass plugs, my net and some other odds and ends; a favorite belt, a wooden box to carry shells . . . homely things whose cost was mainly care and pride.

Time was, and not too long ago, when the magic word was just the other way around—"store-bought." Store-bought was elegance itself; luxury and Sunday Special all rolled into one. Store-bought really meant something that was ordinarily homemade, or could be, that you decided to splurge on.

Store-bought bread, that flimsy modern excuse for food, was once looked on by country folk as something rather special. Don't ask me why. One thing that we tend to forget about homemade is that the cheapest thing a man had to spend in those days was time, and the practiced belief in the old truism that "if you want something done right—do it yourself."

Some of the most lasting and beautiful work in my part of the country exists in our old barns. A farm I once lived on had a barn well over a hundred years old that was still completely in plumb. Not one sagging corner, door or window. Because the man who built it did it right. He selected the full-grown oak. Felled them, and stripped the bark and rolled the felled trees so carefully that they dried straight to start with.

Then with his ax and adze, he cut them square. The keyhole,

the corner joists were all hand-cut and fitted so when the horses raised the timbers a man could ride up on the structure and join it together and know that it would stay that way.

Men were too busy to want to do the same job twice. "Do it once—do it right." I imagine that the same hands that turned a ton of oak into a straight-edge beam could, and did, make their owner's pipes, and whistles for his boys, doll cradles for the little girls, kitchen spoons and chests and chairs. I also imagine that no one else gave his homely skills too much in the way of praise. "Old Eben, he's pretty good with his hands," would have to do for compliments and thanks.

Homemade things are simple things. Stretching boards for schoolboy-caught furs, a bootjack, an inch-thick sweater with the sleeves left too long for accommodating both your growth and the shrinkage of the wool. A milking stool with leather shims under the one leg the maker cut too lean.

These things were never done in haste, but they were done by folks who had other chores to do as well. The mother's hands that knit also milked cows, hoed kitchen gardens, split kindling, kneaded bread—and wielded the switch or hairbrush with the same efficiency and love that bandaged cuts and rubbed away the hurts of growing up.

The men of the house thought nothing of being able to put the set back in a bucksaw, deliver a reluctant calf, spokeshave a hickory limb into an ax handle, and all in the same afternoon.

There were, of course, specialists in things I call "homemade." Certain men were somehow handier at finding where a sick hog hurt, others at fitting a shoe to a plow horse or putting one stone on top of another so it would stay through a winter of freezes and thaws. And there were both local and traveling blacksmiths, harness makers, tinkers and carpenters and stonemasons. But, given the need to have it done now, almost everyone could give almost everything a little better than "a lick and a promise."

14

One of my prized possessions is a handmade, five-tonged fish spear made from an old circular saw blade. The handle was from a long-stemmed hand rake, the kind with whittled wooden teeth.

I got it for several reasons. One, because my grandfather didn't want me using his. Another, because it was easier to get me to collect a mess of fish than it was to get me to help weed the garden or chop wood. And I suspect that Grandpa thought it would please me, and he wasn't above spoiling a boy now and then—especially with the spring air heady with violets and myrtle and a good run of yellow perch and suckers coming up the brook.

I still have my spear, the hand-carved bass plugs, only one of my blacksmith-hammered spoons and a handful of my grandfather's black duck decoys, hand-carved by the man who taught me to plug-cast. Funny, isn't it, how we all seem to have a way of hanging on to handmade things after the store-bought stuff has strayed or been mislaid.

The handmade things I remember were almost always presents. I can't think of anything handmade I know of ever being sold—unless it was for the church or school . . . and more often than not, the stuff that was sold was bought back by the same family. When one of the ladies knit a heavy new sweater you knew she made sure it would fit her Jim or Helen—and Lord help the husband that didn't buy back his own wife's cookies, cakes and pies!

Kids never got charged for anything except store-bought stuff, and even those prices were very flexible, depending on whose boy you were. Our blacksmith spent about half his time fixing wagons, bicycles, traps, riveting belts or whatever and sharpening pocketknives and hatchets. He always let us work the bellows on the forge—which we fought for the privilege of doing as we did over anything he ever allowed us to touch. There was always someone we knew who could make or mend practically anything, and not one of them ever seemed to mind being constantly pestered or ever remarked that our needs were trivial and our constant questions boring and dumb. I suspect they knew we both loved and admired them—and were willing to trade their magic for our questionable company.

There are a lot of things that I suppose you could still call homemade—an Orvis rod, a Loveless or Russell knife, a Pachmayr stock, a Walker reel—but these are really works of art and go beyond what I consider simple country craft.

Handmade is basically something someone does once in a while or now and then, not every day. Not to say that it cannot come out art—because it often does, like my fishing net, or a decoy carved by a ship captain named Joseph Lincoln.

I still like to watch those homemade things come alive in the hands of the makers—a hank of olive yarn turning into a duck-hunting sweater, a chunk of sweet-smelling cedar becoming a top-water plug or a sleeping hen mallard. I am much gentled by things homemade; they seem less busy than commercial goods, and the sounds of a whittling knife in front of a fire will always take me back to other days when time was much more warmly spent.

SNOW

I HOPE you read this when it's snowing.

Somehow snow is nature with its pockets turned inside out—you can see things now that you knew were around . . . but weren't sure exactly where.

The pheasant that scratch for berries under my holly tree stand out like Christmas ornaments against the snow. I can see where the moonlit rabbits danced last night; where the deer reached over the garden fence to nibble the tops off the white-pine seedlings and wonder about the brussels sprouts.

I like to walk in the snow because that's the only time I sound quiet like a woodsman. I like deer stands when it snows because I always think there's something sneaking up on me. I like duck-blinds in the snow because that's the way they look in the old-time pictures I like best.

I like to make snowballs to throw to the Labradors and watch the expression on their faces when they try to catch and retrieve them.

I can walk in unknown places with confidence—because I can always backtrack myself out. And I like the confidence I feel when I see tracks—the side-by-side commas of deer, the feather etching of the grouse or the exclamation point left in the wake of a strutting cock pheasant.

I like the *shush* sound snow makes when it's falling. The sound of friends stamping boots outside before coming in to steam by your fire.

I like the fearsome howl of Western high country blizzards with the wind strumming your tent ropes in long bass notes.

I like to watch the white winds roll up Chesapeake Bay and sheet after sheet pack down the sides of our Alleghenies.

Snow makes me feel elemental, brave and incredibly solitary: a single adventure, alone with only my wits and endurance to help me survive the storm—even if I'm only half a mile away from the car when the first flakes start to fall. It may be only a little adventure—but that's better than no adventure at all.

In the back pocket of my "high-country" coat is a small plastic envelope that holds waterproof matches, a candle stub, a couple of Hershey bars and a tiny stringlike saw. I really don't know whether I ever want to be forced to use them or not, but I suspect that like the kid that enjoys tenting out in his backyard, I'd enjoy a night of midsnow storm survival just where I could barely see the lanterns of the camp. . . .

Ideally there would be, offstage in the darkness, the felt presence of wolves forming an invisible, but known, ring around my blazing campfire—but sensing my absence of fear they would keep their distance. All the well-read know-how of others is stored away for just such an occasion. I would build my fire against a bank of rocks for reflected heat, not under a snow-

burdened evergreen where it would loosen and fall; only ama-
teurs do that. I will have one or two big logs cut for coals, and a
spruce-bough bed that cradles me through the night. The next
morning when I arrive back in camp, no one will have given my
evening a second thought, knowing the depth of my ability to
survive in the snowy wilds. After all, I've been through this a
hundred times—on my half-mile walks back to the car.

Few things are more comforting than to be inside when it's
snowing outside. A bayside shanty with a big pile of dry wood by
the fireplace, plenty of good bourbon and, with luck, some
maple-tree icicles to cool it down. Outside you can hear the
ducks chattering about the plans for tomorrow, and the Lab
stands with her nose pressed against the glass making plans of her
own. Late at night you wake and listen to the wind. Old Tippy
whimpers in her sleep as you pad around and add a log against the
bitter morning.

I'd give a lot to have a day like that expected tomorrow—if
tomorrow were a time that's past that I could choose. I'd like to
pole out in a clear cedar Barnegat sneaker with a dozen or so decoys set around the bow. And if you'd let me choose my ducks,
I'd take wind-driven blacks, those wary spooks that tease and
tease just out of range until the moment that you've given up—
and there they are! There are a lot of places I'd like to hunker in
against the snow—waiting for a chosen tomorrow. A Colorado
meadow tent with a hissing sheepherder's stove and a mule deer
waiting in the aspens. A Michigan farmhouse with the promise of
partridge or a rundown railroad hotel in the prairies where I can
think about sharptails.

Wherever—just add an old friend who understands the kind
of message that we love to read written white-on-white on the
pages of the snow.

THE HORSEMAN

THERE WAS a short period of my life (called youth) when, except for Sunday school and baths, I lived in a cowboy outfit, including furry chaps, gloves and real Western boots sent by my uncle from Oklahoma.

I finally outgrew my costume, and my dreams of becoming a cowboy (which were structured around visions of myself being always long, lean, tanned and wearing *just* the right hat and boots) were sorely restricted in fulfillment by being brought up in an environment that featured an absence of steers and my own lively suspicions regarding the general intelligence and good will of horses.

But my respect for cowboys and Western guides remains as strong as ever. This is due partly to my envy of anyone who lives in such magnificent country, partly because of my constant amazement that these men can always make a horse go in the direction they want and make it stop when they want, and partly because they seem to be the archtypical countrymen who can do anything and do it pretty well.

Fate, which usually leaves me drawing three cards to a low pair, for once turned the other cheek and got me mixed up with an outfitter named Cotton Gordon, from Lake George, Colorado.

Cotton is pretty close to the vision every kid had of himself as a cowboy; he and I hit it off right away and had a fine time discussing six million things about our coming high-country hunt except one crucial point. It never occurred to Cotton, who lives on a horse, that I have limited my relationship to such animals to the occasional $2 bet or, at most, watching the morning workouts at the August meeting at Saratoga with an avaricious eye.

Cotton assumed that everyone knew something, however slight, about riding. I assumed that we would arrive in camp by a method that didn't feature horses. We were both wrong.

The full impact of what lay in store didn't hit until I found myself staring at a string of horses being saddled and packed and heard one of Cotton's hands asking me to walk around and pick out a horse. I laughed and asked him if any of the horses happened to be named Old Maude, Lazybones or anything similar that was descriptive of old age, docility or maidenly virtue. He said no, all the horses were pretty good; Cotton wasn't one of the type that tolerated anything but good horseflesh. I asked him, "Pretty good for what? Casey Tibbs?" He laughed again and pointed to a pile of saddles. He told me to pick one out, with the air of one fine judge of things horsy confiding to another, then went about his work of loading the pack animals.

I took about the same enthusiastic pleasure in choosing a horse and saddle as I would in choosing a time bomb. So I did what any sensible man would do—nothing. I decided to put my

faith in luck and Cotton Gordon. And I was right. Cotton saddled up Sundown, a middle-aged, pleasant-gaited and even-
tempered mare, and led us down the trail that wound toward
camp. The ride itself was fine. The weather was perfect, and
from the top of the mesa we could see the green river valleys below and the snow-capped mountains above. The Colorado air
was a bouquet of late autumn, and now and then we could see
mule deer watching us pass from the edge of the aspens.

The old mare and I were getting along famously. After an
hour or so of timid and questioning indoctrination, our relationship solidified, and I began to believe I was one of those few that
were born to horseback. Sundown and I would canter frivolously
for a few minutes to catch up with the rest of the group. (Lest
you share the same question about the name Sundown that I did,
it referred to her reddish-sunset coloration and not the more
ominous overtones that leapt instantly to my morbid mind.)

I won't say I wasn't relieved to finally see the tents in the distance, but the ride had caused little discomfort in those parts featured in cartoons about beginning horsemen, and my practice
turns and changes of gear were beginning to show some results,
and I felt that Sundown and I had established a good basic mas-
ter/servant relationship.

Cotton from time to time had ridden back to chat and see
how I was getting along, and while I won't say he was visibly impressed, he was at least obviously relieved to note that I hadn't
fallen off or suffered some other catastrophe. We both felt at the
close of our journey that my riding worries were over. We were,
again, both wrong.

I arrived at the hitching rail dead last. Some were casually
unsaddling their horses; others had already finished and were in
their tents unpacking or standing around admiring the view. Cotton was supervising the unloading of the pack horses, organizing
the beginnings of supper, seeing to it that everyone was comfort-

able, telling funny stories and managing to be involved in doing nine or ten things at the same time and doing them all well. I was still on Sundown, who had forgotten me and wandered off into the meadow to graze. I was trying to look as casual as I could—as if the whole scene were purposeful, the faithful steed feeding quietly under the quiet control of her benevolent master.

"Going to join us for supper in the tent or shall I arrange to have you fed up there?" Cotton had finally diagnosed the situation and was standing looking up at me with a quiet smile. "Some folks take to riding right off and can't get enough of it," he went on, "but you sure are one of the most dedicated I've ever seen!"

"Cotton," I whispered, "I can't get off."

"What do you mean you can't get off?" he said in a voice laden with disbelief. "You don't know how—or you don't want to?"

"I want to get off about as much as anything I ever wanted in my life," I told him, "but I can't move my right leg. I can't throw it over the saddle."

"Well then, can you move your left leg and get off the other side? I hate to have to shoot old Sundown just to get you on the ground."

The fact that a horse has two sides had never occurred to me, and while Cotton held the horse still, I slid off and began hobbling around. When he finished tying her up and removing the tack he asked me how I felt.

"Fine," I told him. "Must have been a little catch in a muscle."

Cotton went on to tell me how even the most experienced riders sometimes got a little catch like that, but I'd be fine tomorrow. And after Cotton's steak supper, I took a little walk and went over to see Sundown for a chat. To my surprise, I did feel fine.

Cotton's the kind of outfitter who runs a happy camp. He's a good cook, and a nonstop storyteller who only pauses long enough to laugh at a tale of yours. So by bedtime, I'd nearly forgotten the fact that I had an early-morning date with Sundown. My mind was on mule deer and trying to remember a golf story to top one Cotton had broken up the camp with. But the next morning found the kid who liked to play cowboy all played out.

From where I sat resting my leg I could look out over the little brook that ran through the foot of the camp and see the great West repeating itself—mountain after mountain separated by vast meadows and low woodlands.

In the distance across the valley some of our pack horses were working out their own kinks, rolling in the soft meadow grass like so many russet puppies. I could hear them playing and could imagine the men that first tamed this massive country sitting, in times past, around a camp a bit like mine and thinking not in terms of distance that they had to travel but in terms of time— weeks and months that spread out between Denver, and some tiny ranch house they might call home.

I remembered their lonesome songs created to help pretend they had a name other than Pete or Red and friends who knew it.

I thought I'd just sit there for a morning, keep the fire working, rest my leg and think. Maybe the West will grow a little smaller for me as time goes by. I'd like to get comfortable with this country . . . but a man has to grow into it . . . he has to learn to sing the lonesome songs before this kind of country looks like home.

CHAMPIONS AND US

A CASUAL FRIEND of mine, who had been liberally sipping on my good bourbon, got kidding me about my *Sports Afield* columns and said that I was being far too humble and modest about my shooting ability.

I fooled with that for a minute and resisting the temptation to agree, told him that maybe to him I was an adequate shot when the moon was in the right phase and Taurus was ascending or whatever, but to the good shots I'm nothing . . . well . . . maybe better than nothing, but not a lot.

Good shooting is a lot like good dog work in that most people never get a chance to see the best. I don't mean a man that can go out and break an occasional twenty-five or even a hundred at trap or skeet, I mean a man who goes out and breaks a hundred just about every time—rain or shine, hot weather or cold, windy or calm and whether he really feels top-hole or not. And believe me, there are a lot around.

I've got a Canadian friend who has been on an Olympic trap team and has been a world champion at Olympic skeet—that's gun down with birds so fast it's quite possible to have a referee call a target "lost" simply because you didn't see it. He has also come home with more money than he left with after taking on the best Europeans at live-pigeon matches in Spain and France. And I can name quite a few like him—including some that he considers to be a bit better than he is!

There are men and women around who look like champions just getting the gun out of its case. I went up to watch a live-pigeon match in Pennsylvania a couple of months ago where one of the best shots I know was shooting. The weather was below freezing with a wind gusting up to 30 mph, and my friend never missed a bird. One of the other bystanders remarked that Frank didn't seem to draw the real hard flyers that some of the others were missing. And I knew why and told him; Frank was so much faster and so much more accurate that he didn't let the bird have time to get hard to handle.

The fine shots are all like that. They bring a quality of aggressiveness to their shooting that lets them master the situation where the average gunner lets the game, or circumstances, master him.

A first-rate shot has a combination of poise, timing and concentration so well under control that he stays "on top" of the game, a little longer than most. He always shoots with style.

I recently watched a young man casually run a hundred skeet targets in pretty bad weather and was impressed enough to mention that I thought he was more than a fair hand with a shotgun. An older shooter, a many-time champion himself, smiled at me and said, "Yes, he is a pretty fair shot—but he's not a champion, and he never will be." I was more than a little surprised at that and asked for a clearer explanation. "A champion has to beat other champions," he said. "He has to want to be top dog, and he has to be comfortable way up there by himself. This young fellow has a fear of winning. He really doesn't want to beat the name boys in the sport. He doesn't want the reputation of being the man everybody else has to beat. Maybe it's embarrassment, maybe it's something else . . . but he's really just another fine shot, nothing more."

Hemingway once defined bravery as "grace under pressure." And that would suit me fine as a description of a champion. The real tangible pressures of a major shoot start long before you fire the first shot. Take a major skeet match, for example. A double-A gun knows before he leaves home that he will be expected to break 200 straight in the 12-gauge and then another 100 or so at doubles at all stations in the shoot-off for anyone to know he's even been there. At the Grand American Trapshoot in Vandalia, Ohio, this summer I can guarantee that quite a few men will have run 500 or more targets without a miss . . . in front of crowds, in the rain, in near-darkness, shooting against the best-of-the-best, under pressure. And somebody has to win. Somebody will falter for a split second in a long shoot-off after they've broken 200 straight and have to step down. He'll walk off the line with a smile, his head held proudly, and with at most maybe a shrug of the shoulders in the way of an excuse. But you'll hear no small complaints, no biting remarks, no blame . . . because he's a champion, and he knows he'll be back in another shoot-off after another 200 straight.

I think that the proven champions, the Rosettis, the Britt Robinsons, the Elgin Gateses, the Orlichs, the Don Johnsons, the Punkin Flocks, are incredible athletes. They withstand daily the pure punishment of at least 200 rounds of shooting; often much more. Then they go into the overtime rounds. Someone wins gratefully; someone loses, regretfully. And tomorrow they go do the same thing all over again. That's courage, strength and a dedicated sense of purpose matched to an incredible skill. Win or lose, they smile. That's grace under pressure.

Maybe one of the reasons I like winners is that as F. Scott Fitzgerald once said of the rich, "They are different than you or me."

And I am glad to report that all the really fine shooters I know are gentlemen or ladies and always more than kind and helpful to their lesser-gifted kin. Some years back I was lucky enough to win some lowly class or other at a fairly large trap-shoot, and while I was struggling with my prize, my guns and shells and sweaters and other gear, a voice behind me said, "Here son, let me help you, I wouldn't want to see you drop your trophy . . . I'd be real proud of that if I were you." He took a ton of duffel from me and walked a long way with me to my car and helped me put the stuff away. He didn't know me from Adam's off-ox. But I knew who he was. I'd just watched him break one of the rare hundred-straights in trap doubles, then go out and win the shoot-off for High-All-Around. He was a champion—in more ways than one. I doubt if John Sternburger remembers me, but I remember him with a great deal of respect.

I like all shooters, really. And I can honestly say from the likes of us to the likes of them, that you can't find a nicer group of people in the country. I like the games of trap and skeet, I like the look of the guns worn white from use and care. I like the talk around a gun club and the smell of powder and gun oil. I like the feeling of excitement in the pit of my stomach when the gun locks shut for the first shot. I like the feeling of optimism that I almost always have before I start, and I've come to accept the inevitable fate of what will be the results when I'm finished . . . with some optimism left for the next time.

Shooting really doesn't have any "losers." When the match is done, the lost shots taken one more time in front of the fire, and we've said our goodbyes to old friends we always leave with that special feeling of warmth after a day that only comes when you know you've been in the right place, with the right people measuring yourself against a very basic scale—and finding out you weren't so bad after all.

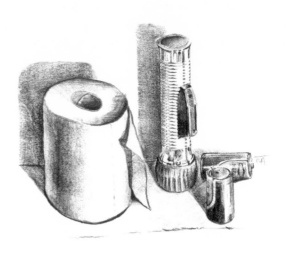

FLASHLIGHTS

THERE ARE several schools of thought on what constitutes the greatest modern contribution to our society. Some hold for aluminum foil, some for plastic wrap; I stand solidly with those who vote for the flashlight.

I don't know who invented the flashlight, but I can imagine him thinking, "Fine, everyone who wants one will buy it, maybe two. And now all he has to do is replace a battery now and then and occasionally a bulb. Not a great business, but not a bad business."

How wrong he was! It seems to me that the individual flashlights I've owned have had individual characters. Some never work. Others work at odd times, and the majority hide and disappear moments after being brought into the house. The solution to all this, as far as I can tell, is a perfect revelation of the American attitude: It turns out to be easier, and nearly cheaper, to continue to buy new flashlights than it is to buy batteries or bulbs. It is also consistently inconsistent in that the old flashlights are never thrown out, if found, until they start leaking a viscous fluid of greenish tinge. It is at this moment, when the flashlight has obviously ridden the pale horse, that the American sportsman does his best to save it. The exuding batteries are chiseled out, the tube flushed with bicarbonate of soda and scrubbed while all the other flashlights in the house watch. It is, of course, of no use and after several attempts at exchanging batteries between other flashlights and the lost one, it is finally tossed into a drawer. But it is never totally forgotten or put on the junk heap where it belongs.

A flashlight represents some sort of ancient magic, a rekindling of our fascination with fire. I wouldn't say we actually worship the flashlight—but we secretly come pretty close. And, as we all know, each flashlight seems to exhibit some kind of reasoning power. There is the flashlight that cannot be abruptly snapped on; the switch must be eased into the "on" position as if taking the whole machine by surprise. Others must be smartly whacked against a tree or a door edge before they relinquish one yellow, fading gleam. There are those that work perfectly around the house in the prepacking-testing period and then stay completely dark in the camp only to glow brightly again when brought home to the company of 150-watt table lamps.

I have not yet stooped to pretending, in front of a flashlight, that I don't give a damn whether it works or not in order to make it function out of its perverse nature, but I've come perilously close to it; especially with those demons of my coon-hunting youth—the eight- and ten-battery monsters, advertised to "light up a coon's eyes up to a quarter of a mile away." I tried quite a few kinds, at great expense, but slowly and surely I realized that the number of batteries cubed the odds against the thing ever working. And after a long night stumbling into barbed wire, reeling piteously from stepping into a hole that might have made a decent well, and all the while staggering under the weight of five pounds of nonflashing flashlights, I would go back to the hardware store and find, to no one's surprise, after using the little testing machine, that all the batteries as well as the bulb were in A-Number-1 condition, even if I was not. Always the optimist, I would rub emery cloth on the contact points, pull the spring in the cap out even farther and find that the light would work fine—until I needed it.

I finally realized that I had no need (or chance) of seeing a coon's eyes a quarter of a mile away and compromised by carrying several two- or three-battery lights in my hunting coat. Every once in a while one of them would actually throw a beam that you could see a coon's eyes in—a full ten to thirty feet away. One learns to compromise in the face of reality.

It was necessary, in my younger days, to not even attempt sleep unless the comforting hardness of a flashlight was felt under the pillow. This flashlight was something special, a most prized possession, and was under no circumstances ever lent. Not only was it protection against "the things that go bump in the night," but it was a down-to-earth must for calls of nature that led to the small house at the edge of the orchard.

The pillow-flashlight got its toughest workout, however, in reading when you were supposed to be asleep. First of all, its beam was rarely strong enough to be seen through two layers of blankets, and if you were alert enough to survive anything in those days, you could always switch it off before anybody caught you late at night. Reading late was frowned on for two reasons: One, the pitiful lemony light was supposed to be bad for your eyes, and second, if you stayed up all night reading you were bound to stumble drowsily through your chores the next day, or worse commit the ultimate, unpardonable crime of falling asleep during arithmetic or geography class.

But there were few nights that passed without reading from

one of the sporting magazines about an adventure in the frozen North or the brain-scorching heat of Africa. Lacking that, I was a thorough fan of *G-8 and His Battle Aces,* any baseball story and the usual assortment of Tom Swift, the Rover Boys and the like.

There is something delicious about reading, surreptitiously, in bed by flashlight. A mini-adventure of a kind that provided a better appreciation of a tale of danger or hardship than any no-glare, easy-on-the-eyes, recommended-by-doctors electric light.

I guess I still have to classify myself as a flashlight freak. I counted the other day, and I have eleven around the house, including two rechargeables that no one ever remembers to plug in. Of the nine remaining, six have no batteries, one has batteries but doesn't work, and the other two are the throw-away kind that have worked fine for over two years in spite of the fact that they aren't supposed to. I do not count the big one-battery kind; I have three of those, but they never work, and I've quit buying batteries and hoping—but I just can't throw them away.

As you know, no one is more hopeful than a born loser. I have my eye on a couple of the new lights advertised as one kind or another of "electric lantern," bringing the whole business back full circle to where it started years and years ago.

The most important move in keeping your own flashlight, when you find one that's sympathetic, is to hide it from the kids. Easier said than done, right? And remembering my own unerring instincts I applied psychology rather than rely on a loose floorboard or a secret panel and bought each of the girls their own flashlight, showed them how to replace the bulbs and batteries and bought extras of those. You can guess what happened—I have no personal flashlight, nor do they.

Even harder than keeping a flashlight in the house is keeping one that will work in the car. That is about the first flashlight anyone will borrow, because that's the one flashlight that everyone knows the location of. If it is not stolen by your flesh and blood, it's forgotten, and the batteries will leak acid all over the good screwdriver and pliers you left along with it in the glove compartment.

As for other "special" flashlights, those for the fishing-tackle box, the duck-hunting kit or the deer camp, forget it. I have and happily—I simply buy a new one every time I think I need it now and, oddly enough, more often than not, they work—often for several days at a time, and frequently when I really need them.

You probably remember a series of advertisements proclaiming the virtue of a particular brand of flashlight batteries (virtues that I have no reason to doubt in the flashlights of others). This heroic flashlight featured lifesaving signals that summoned help from great distances in times of ultimate crisis. My flashlights could only be used to summon help by Morse code— and not by flashing three dots and three dashes to rescuers searching far off in the dark, but only by using the butt end to pound heavily on a wall.

I think that I shall never see
A flashlight that always works for me.
A torch who when its switch is on
Sends forth its light to part of gloom.
No burning sun do I require—but a simple
Beam to lead 'twixt path and mire.

A torch that when I need to travel
Distinguishes between sea and gravel.
When to the outhouse I must go, a light
That guides me in its yellow glow.

Stories are written by fools like me
Who grope and stumble and cannot see
For those of you who are forever blest
With a guiding light whenever "on" is prest.

TIMES PAST ON
THE EASTERN SHORE

My DAYS SPENT on the Eastern Shore are all too few. And no matter how good the gunning ever is, the memory of how it used to be makes my "three dead in the air" seem a mockery of what the word "waterfowling" used to mean to the men of the Chesapeake Bay.

I've listened to the old-timers wistfully recalling the nights they took ducks outlined in flight against the full of an ice-white moon. I've heard them talk about the sinkboxes surrounded by more than three hundred decoys and how they would lie there wet, frozen and often frightened of a running sea and a ten-knot wind. I've heard the baymen talk softly among themselves about the live tollers, blacks and mallards and Canadas, that they used to train. I've seen their guns from "0" bores to the "little" 10-gauge side-by-side. Yes, I've listened to the talk and seen their boats and held their guns, but I know nothing of the meaning of their words.

I will never see the thousands upon thousands of canvasbacks on opening day along the Susquehanna flats. I will never thread a boat, shipping water from the weight of mallards, with a sculling oar at one end and a gunning light at the other.

I will never know the bellow of a half-pound of sixes tamped down in front of black powder and oakum. I'll not likely take in my lifetime as many as some of these men have often taken in a single day.

They tell of the nights so filled with music; the whistling of pintails, the grunting of geese, the tuk-tuk of mallards that two men in a blind had to talk to each other by kicking and poking.

They let me hear their words, but it is really to each other that they talk of another time—and not to me.

I will never know their Currituck, their Pamlico, their Nags Head, their Smith and Tangiers islands.

But the one thing I know is their mind. I can imagine what it must have been like to set out with a case of handmade shells and expect, on a very good day, to use the whole batch up. And I wish I could have done it—just one time.

They—the old gunners and baymen—talk about the hardness. They talk about the cold and the wet and the days that came and went without sleep, and I see their hands and I understand. Hands that lived in ice and around oars and push-poles and rope and frozen netting and hatchets, draw knives and files. Hands that brought canvasbacks and ruddies and brant alive from cedar logs. Hands that crafted deadeyes, and sneak-skiffs and pungeys. Hands that tell me more of what they're saying than the words.

But it's the eyes that give them away. It's the looking backward to the day they stared down the barrel of an old Remington

Model 11 with a ten-shot extension on the magazine more than five hundred times a day—on more days than one. And I see an excitement there that I wish I'd known firsthand—just once.

We are the same, these old men and me. Separated a bit by time and fortune, but imagination stirs my gunning blood the same—and when I close my eyes I can see it all . . . I can feel the cold, duck-riding wind on the back of my neck. My hands, still frozen from helping set out more than a hundred blocks, are tucked up in my armpits for warmth. I would have had my 10-gauge hammer gun reamed out about to almost cylinder bore for the first shot, and a touch more choke for the second. It is still night, the reluctant winter sun imperceptible yet behind the heavy banks of scudding clouds that promise snow before noon. But I can hear them overhead pouring through the dark from sheltered bays on the first flights to the flats where wild celery grows. And I wait—not for any legal shooting time, but just for light enough to silhouette the sculpture of the canvasback over a gun barrel.

And at last, as it always must, it happens. I have heard the cans dropping in among the decoys for the last half-hour and now with light, I stand and shoot. Three fall with the first barrel as they blossom up from the water and then a pair of drakes tumble with the second. (I always shoot beautifully in my imagination.)

And as fast as I can load and shoot they drive in to the stool. My pick-up man is standing by until I'm done—and by the time the other working men are at their jobs, I'm through.

Ducks of all sorts nearly brush our caps as we retrieve and pick up the handmade decoys from the freezing chop. Who could have ever stood there then and guess that in less than thirty years these skies would be near silent and a box of shells would last the average gunner for a month? Who would then have ever said that his great-grandchildren would likely never know the smell of roasting canvasback and a daily limit of other ducks could be carried in just one hand?

I can't find it in myself to condemn the old-time gunners. It is indeed a tragedy that they did not realize the havoc that they wrought—but a tragedy born of ignorance rather than intent. And lest we too hastily blame them for being ignorant, let me remind you of the atomic clouds that still circle the atmosphere, DDT, thalidomide, leaded gasoline, mercury wastes, phosphates, just to name a few—that in the last years have done more to affect our living environment than the short span of time that was the heyday of the commercial gunner.

And what about you? I'd like to bet that I could find you any morning of the gunning season dressing in your union suit of scratchy wool by the light of a smoky kerosene lantern. Your good wife downstairs in the kitchen making oatmeal, some fried home-cured ham and a blue enamel pot of boiled coffee, and maybe a buttermilk biscuit or two to tamp the whole thing down. Along about half-past three, with the second cup of coffee in your hand, you'd be out on the porch smelling the wind like an eager hound. Your wife sees the timeless excitement in your face and takes pleasure in the fact there's still a lot of boy that's living in the man she married years ago. I hope she'll be the one to hear my horse's hooves striking sparks from the frozen road and come out to say hello when I stop to pick you up—with a hot cup and maybe a biscuit or two.

You take the reins while I light my pipe and tuck Old Maude's blanket in a little tighter around my knees; seems the mornings are a little brisker than they used to be. The horse forces herself into a tiny trot, pretending she's as excited as we are, and we just sit there staring at the cold blue sky—not saying much, just sort of puffing our pipes at each other as certain men are apt to do when they know for sure that there's no place in the world they'd rather be.

Give Maude a little flick of the reins; it won't do much good, but it flatters her.

THE RINGNECK HUNTER

I'm a ringneck hunter, can't you tell?
My pants are torn, my face is scratched and my nerves are shot
    to hell.

I've hunted duck and I've hunted quail and I think they're lots of
    fun,
But until I said hello to Mr. Ringneck my gunning hadn't begun.

"Oh, come and hunt the cockbirds," my hunting buddies cried,
"He's an easy shot, and good for the pot
And a pretty thing beside.
For even a dog that's blind he's easy to find
In the cornfields and the swamp.
Come, take just one and if it isn't fun
You can go right back to camp."

The first bird I saw was fifty yards and running like a deer.
The next three or four were just as far—but they were in the air.
My quail-trained dog just looked at me and said, "This isn't fair!"

"Hie on, Old Sue," I shouted, "he's just another bunch of
    feathers;
If we don't get the first or so we'll surely get the others."
Now the rooster doesn't fly too far and he doesn't fly too fast,
So Sue and I had marked them down—they were ours at last!

The dog snuck in and so did I, it was a little cedar clump,
We've got you now, I said out loud, and slipped the safety up,
One bird went east, and one went west and one flew right at me,
By the time I made my mind up . . . they were gone behind the
    tree.
"That's one for them, Old Sue," I said, "but I've got them
    figured out.
You just run right in, the next time; I know now what they're
    about,
They'll flush a little out in front and that's just where I will be,
They're not that smart and if we do our part it'll be one up for
    you and me."

Well, the whole thing worked the way I thought—but again he
    had us beat,
The bird I swore would flush out *there* came up between my feet!

He runs on me, he hides on me, he sneaks by me on the sly,
He waits until I've passed him before he tries to fly.

He laughs at me, he mocks my dog, he leads me into briars,
He's always where I think he's not,
He's turned my best friends into liars.

THE RINGNECK HUNTER

That's the way it's been with me, although I've got a few,
I've become a ringneck hunting fool—and I don't think there's
   any cure.
My pants are torn, my face is scratched and my nerves are shot
   to hell.
But I'm learning Mr. Ringneck . . . and I'm learning him quite
   well.
No matter what I think he'll do, odds are he'll prove me wrong,
But the frosty wind's the music and his cackles are the songs
That lead me to the cornfields and the swamps where he belongs.

I think every man finds just the bird that suits him down the line,
It's bobwhite for some, and grouse for some . . . but Mr. Smarty-
   pants is mine!

LOGIC VS. WIVES

SOME TIME AGO, I made a little mistake. Unintentionally, perhaps, but nevertheless, a mistake. This was in the form of an article about some of the ways I have resorted to in order to sneak a new gun into a household already creaking with the weight of locks, stocks and barrels.

Well, the whole thing has gotten out of control—and worse, the wives of the guilty have learned to read. Two recent extremes have been brought to my attention: One is a man who has, in the past few years, sneaked over three hundred guns into his home. He sneaked a lot of them out, and sold them in order to make room for the new, of course, but the reason behind all this massive coming-and-going was mainly the thrill, the challenge, the deviousness required to sneak them in past his wife. That became the whole reason. He doesn't really care about guns, per se, being content to shoot rats at the dump with an old bolt-action .410.

One realizes that to be adroit enough to sneak hundreds of guns past a wife with the watch-dog qualities of Cerberus, the guardian dog of Hades, requires more than a little theatrical sense and almost unbelievable chicanery. I won't, of course, divulge all of his secrets and methods, since my wife also has learned to read since I started shooting trap and the odd duck and quail; I can always use another gun myself.

I will only mention that a new Perazzi arrived wrapped in twenty yards of hall carpeting—and since his wife was anxious for a new rug, the gun move was almost second-nature for the swift-thinking collector. New full-length cushions for the patio furniture came in boxes that also carried a Ruger M-77 in .30-06, a 1-in-1000 Remington 3200 Trap, and a mint Iver Johnson Skeeter. Obvious to you and me—but to the woman of the house eager to have done with chair pads that she's been patching with electrician's tape, not all that obvious. While we might look in the trunk of a new car, would your wife do so immediately if the car were the same deep blue as the color of her eyes?

Not quite so lucky was a correspondent who essayed the "old shotgun that I'm going to make into a lamp" gambit, only to find that the next day his wife had wired and fitted a three-way bulb into a brand-new Ithaca Century.

Let's assume that for years you've been shooting a Krieghoff over-and-under trap gun. You decide, rightly enough, that you need a backup just in case something unusual happens. The backup you have in mind is a Winchester 101 single-barrel. Now since your wife is neither blind nor stupid, she will instantly note that the guns are different. One has two barrels, the other only one. You are now in a bind of your own making. The wealthy gunner avoids this by buying a *second* Krieghoff identical or close enough to the first one to keep the opposing party guessing; the

rest of us must rely on our wits. Since trapshooters are well
known to be above the average waterline of intelligence, this is
not too difficult. (I assume that the wife in question is not a
trapshooter too, which raises another whole set of problems that I
hope to cope with later, if I ever figure it out.)

Years ago, before Women's Lib, when kitchens didn't have
dishwashers, television and radio, and women went to bed at the
decent hour of seven p.m., pleasantly tired from the healthy pur-
suits of chopping stovewood, putting up two hundred jars of pre-
serves and spinning wool into yarn, the lady of the house didn't
sass the master about trivialities. But now that the rosy-cheeked
farm girls of yesterday are into politics, dry martinis and store-
bought frocks, they no longer wait to speak until spoken to. (My
own wife has recently stopped referring to me as "Mr. Hill" and
now uses the familiar "Gene" for address even in public.)

Well, back to your standing in the kitchen, with two dis-
similar guns, on the way to spending a quiet and restful Sunday at
the gun club. Your wife says, "Is that *another* new gun?" Ignore
the law of nature that requires women to refer to any gun in
terms of it being *new, another,* or *expensive;* they can't help it.

First off—do not try to use logic or reasoning. Women like
stories, and you must be prepared to tell her a good one. Keep it
simple, because she'll remember it *exactly,* word for word, and
you may have to repeat it every so often. Keep it light in tone,
and a touch of humor never hurts—remember that loud talk in the
morning will affect you adversely later when you're on Stations
One and Five.

A basic good story can be centered around another woman
that your wife is not overly fond of, and that the 101 in question
is something that her husband asked you to pick up for him and
deliver to the gun club. Implied in this is the idea that the other
wife is not as kind and understanding as yours. Basic—but solid.

You must remember that it is not necessary that your wife

actually *believe* the story, chapter and verse, only that it be *believable* when she repeats it while cutting up the woman she isn't fond of in the first place.

Another theme is woven around the bit that the gun actually belongs to Ralph who wants you to try it out for him since he isn't a first-rate shot and isn't sure where it's shooting. Bring out that Ralph isn't at the gun club much because *his* wife makes him stay home most Sundays to do chores. Implied here is that your wife is several cuts above Ralph's in charity. If this seems to get a good reception, you can build on it by hinting that such restrictions on Ralph vis-à-vis the gun club are not having too good an effect on his marriage.

Try not to answer specific questions about the other wives: the cost of the gun or has Ralph been seeing anyone else on the side. Make your story brief and move out. Timely repetitions of these stories when necessary will allow you to be seen with the 101 until she's no longer aware that it's new. Now you have both an over-and-under and a single-barrel, and new additions of either configuration can be disguised as "that same old gun I've had for years, I just cleaned it up."

Listen to the other men at the club. Remember their stories. Keep track of the harmony, or lack of it, in their marriages, jobs, etc. You never know when you're going to stumble over a sensational bargain.

For reasons I don't understand, fishermen never have these problems. Wives think that all guns are expensive and that all rods cost less than $10 and reels and lines are thrown in. A friend of mine has a priceless collection of Leonards, Paynes and Paul Youngs—with a Walker reel for each—and is forced to leave the house with a hammer gun he bought mail-order when he was a kid. He has a couple of goodies he locks in the safe at the club that he actually shoots, but he's denied the deep pleasure of cleaning and handling them at home. We have discussed trading an

old wooden rod, as his wife calls them, for one of my old guns—
but he feels that a man can't live with just one good gun around,
and if he ends up with several alongside his fly rods, he might begin to be asked some very hard questions.

I know that a lot of you newlywed shooters want to tell me
that "Pauline isn't like that; she's different. She understands." Let
me assure you of a couple of things about Pauline. In spite of her
marks in U.S. history in school, Pauline, like all wives, has acquired total recall. In ten years you will no doubt be a little hazy
about what you did on Saturday, May 18, 1974. But Pauline will
know; that was the day you had promised to drive up to her
mother's but you forgot and stayed at the gun club until long after dark and made her overcook the roast and scorch the rissolé
potatoes, and she was wearing that cute little green dress that she,
up until that time, thought you liked so much. Pauline, who you
thought believed that three plus three equals seven, will be able to
estimate to four decimals the money you spend on shooting, dogs
and related frivolities.

Other men who believe, as I do, that their Queen Bee is the
sweetest apple on the tree of happiness have figured, "What the
hell, I spend so much time gunning and whatever, I'll just get the
QB her own gun. She might enjoy it." Strong men I know now
weep at the reminder of the day they brought home a Diana
Grade with a short stock and took their fragile wives to the club—
cautioning them about the noise and the recoil and the problems
of left angles from Station Two.

A year later—and this has happened to us all—you arrive
home expecting to be greeted by the soft odor of freshly baked
bread and a little chit-chat about what went on at the manse. You
embrace your life's partner and find that she is redolent of gunpowder and Hoppes No. 9. You ask her how things are, and she
starts telling you, target by target, about how she ran the first 25,
why she dropped two on the second field, and if Suzy can show

up every once in a while with a new trap gun, why can't she? There's this cute little Ithaca she saw at the gunsmith's when she went to pick up a case of shells, and what would be wrong with shortening the stock on your Model 12 because you hardly ever shoot it any more anyway . . .

Now when we get a new rug or some patio cushions delivered—I'm the one checking the contents for Perazzis. Just the other day someone asked me how Marcia was, and without thinking I said, "Fine, but she's having a little trouble on Station Five."

H. L. Mencken once said, "No man is genuinely happy, married, who has to drink worse whiskey than he used to drink when he was single." I guess that as long as that applies to our shotguns, we're still okay.

ICE FISHING

ONE OF THE REASONS I have remained so ignorant of so many of the things going on around me is that I spend so much of my time staring up in the sky or peering down trying to make out what's going on in the water.

It was a natural thing that I should take to ice fishing; it's one of the most perfect outdoor pastimes for a born loafer. Where else can you spend most of your time rotating your carcass around a good fire, scorching and steaming in turn, and looking down through a hole watching for fish and still look busy?

Besides the active loafing, ice fishing had a lot going for it. First there was the discussing stage that covered where, weather and the general preparation. The next step was to put the chains on the Model A. That was one of my jobs because, for reasons I don't remember, one rear tire was a little larger than the other—

so if the first set of chains went on relatively easy you knew you had the wrong chain on the wrong wheel. A really successful job of getting chains on always left you wet, frozen and with bleeding fingers—there was a lot of satisfaction in that job I can assure you; when it was finished you felt and looked like you'd been doing something! The second phase was going out to look for bait. We were particular about getting the right kind of shiners and getting the right size. Most people used saltwater killies, but we felt that they weren't big enough, lively enough or hardy enough. It had to be fresh-caught local shiners. And you had to go looking for them. We had a telephone of sorts, but it didn't matter much whether it worked or not since almost no one else had one anyway. We'd go out driving around and buy six or eight here and maybe a dozen someplace else—each and every one discussed and handpicked. I know it sounds crazy, but I had "pet" shiners that I wouldn't let anyone else use. They just looked better to me.

Pop always scorned store tip-ups as extravagant and impractical and inefficient. Instead, we cut sticks of lakeside willow or alder about two feet long, made a little slit under the bark, and after sounding the water, slipped the line under the slit, so the shiner would be as deep as we wanted it, and tied a little piece of red rag in the line below the slit. When a fish took the bait the red flag simply disappeared, and we knew we had a bite. Further, if it simply got too cold or we stayed out on the lake too long we just left the sticks in the ice.

Every so often I got fancy ideas and would make a few tip-ups out of lattice board and old corset stays, but I really liked the little willow sticks a lot more. I don't remember ever seeing anyone else use the kind of setup we liked, and I've always wondered why. They were foolproof, free and a lot easier to move and carry. And they kind of made you feel a little bit like you were living off the land—or could if you really had to.

49

The only hard part was cutting holes. My bad reputation about being careless with edged tools carried well over to the old ax we used for fishing through the ice, so I almost never had to cut the holes. Further was the argument about how big the hole should be. I leaned toward optimism, and if I was allowed to cut my own holes they turned out to be about three feet across. Not only was that sheer fantasy but somewhat dangerous, and it took me so long to cut a hole that big I'd never have gotten more than five or six lines in. And the old ice ax was the only thing we ever used—no matter how thick the ice. You often got wet using it on the last few inches of really thick ice, but it did a nice neat job, and somehow it seemed important to have it look just right.

Our lines were heavy cord; I seem to remember that we used plumb-line and dyed it green. Each line was about fifteen feet or a bit more in length with a hook on one end and a loop on the other. The hook of one line fastened through the loop of another and the whole business of twenty or so lines was (being in one piece so to speak) wrapped around a big notched board with a rope handle for carrying. I figure that the whole business, so far, had to cost less than a dollar. The only other extras were the red rags, a dipsy sinker for sounding and an old wire strainer we used for skimming the ice out of the holes as they froze. The whole business was carried in a wicker basket, with the blue quart Thermos full of tea with honey riding on top.

As soon as the holes were cut and lines set out I was itching to build the fire. And you have to know that the kind of kid who would cut a three-foot hole to catch a pickerel you could pull up through a jug would have to build a fire so big and hot no one could get near it. If all the wet mittens I burned up trying to dry them were laid out end to end—I'd deny it!

I usually ate my lunch before nine o'clock simply because I liked getting exactly the right toasting stick cut and couldn't wait to use it. I never cared too much for toasted onion sandwich, really, but there was a strong belief going around in those days that raw onions kept you from all sorts of dread diseases. I never contracted any dread diseases—so who knows? If being wet and cold was unhealthy I never would have seen the ripe old age of twelve.

So here we are. It's ten in the morning. On the shoreline roars a hardwood fire . . . and spread out in some loose formation that is intended to cover varying depths of water (my favorite set or two in the deepest part where I was wrongly convinced the big ones dwelt) and *nothing* happening. Time to skim the holes and jig the shiners just a bit to wake things up. And somehow, in all this random world, one hole would assume a special something to my eye. I'd sneak my favorite shiner on that one hook—and watch the red rag like a hawk. Then, before too long, I'd find myself with my hat brim in the water, hands shading my eyes just so—and watching what went on underneath in that dark and lambent world. A world as fascinating—or maybe more—than anything I've ever seen. A world of cold shadows. A world of infinite mystery where I could imagine pickerel the size of oars and bass as big as hip boots.

But happily, it is more often than not the fish that are never seen that keep us coming back to fish again. Real fish are not the ultimate fish, no matter how big—we are convinced that deep down there swims something bigger.

The great thing about fishing is that we almost never know. And all we really learn from peering down through our hole in the ice is the everlasting magic of simple wonder.

The last set of willow sticks we ever used is sitting in a bundle tied with binder twine in a very special corner of my room. A faded picture of my father cleaning pickerel on the ice hangs right beside them. The rest is lost—except the hollow thunk-thunk sound of the ax biting into ice, the still-young happiness that comes with staring into a dark-green world that I will never understand and seeing the old plumb-line go taut and, as if by magic, comes the charging monster pickerel that still lives there, beneath the ice—a dream that is as new and old as fishing is itself.

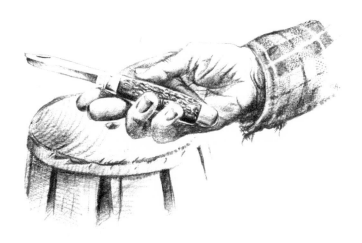

POCKETKNIVES

When I was a kid (how regretfully I write that phrase . . .) no
self-respecting boy over seven would be caught outside of his
nightshirt without a pocketknife. And the knife was used at every
opportunity. We ignored the sharpener that came in our pencil
boxes (remember the pencil box that came with compartments
and trays?) and sharpened our pencils with the pocketknife—
being very careful not to waste too much of the pencil. We made
whistles. And toothpicks. And carved our initials in the school-
yard trees. We cut our sandwiches in quarters, and of course
played mumblety-peg during our fifteen-minute recess. (Could
you still do a "nose-y"?) In my one-room schoolhouse a single
teacher taught seven grades—and contrary to too many of today's
schools, our teacher not only assumed each of the boys, and some
of the girls, carried a knife, she counted on it.

53

The only problem that I had was the fact that by the time my grandfather or father gave me a knife they had completely worn it out. And when I say completely, I mean just that. Both men were semi-professional trappers when they weren't farming. So between skinning (they also bought furs—frequently unskinned) and the constant sharpening and the day-in-and-day-out use a knife got around a farm, an ordinary blade was in short order reduced to the general shape and usefulness of a toothpick. About all that was left was the groove in the back for your thumbnail to open it with. Then and only then was it given to me. I treasured them well enough, but what I really wanted was a knife of my own. A new knife. A nice, bright, sharp, full-bladed knife with a horn handle and a metal loop that we tied an old shoelace over for the times we carried the knife in the front pocket of the bib overalls. There was a buttonhole in the bib that the lace fastened through. A lot of the men carried their big round pocket watches the same way. (We called those big brass-cased Elgins and Ingersolls "turnips.")

There were several reasons I didn't have my own knife. Economic; the fact that I was careless and always losing stuff and that old country attitude so well summed up in the phrase that the knives I had were "good enough." But the only thing they were good enough for was the fact that I could never get one really sharp and nobody worried too much about my cutting my fingers off with one. When Pop gave me a knife it was really more of a souvenir of times past than a knife. You didn't cut with it—you sort of sawed.

As the years passed all of us country boys got more and more used to hand-me-downs—knives included—and wishes faded into the more practical problems of how to cope with reality. As a grown man with a family I still was heir to my father's worn-out knives, and when I got to the point where I could stretch another year or so out of it a pocketknife became a symbol of something that I came to regard with deep affection—if I didn't lose it.

The grown men all had one big knife each. A hunting knife. It was used sparingly, only for skinning deer and the farm animals we butchered. It seems to me that they spent as much or more time sharpening them as they did using them—but somehow they never got worn out to the point where I ever inherited one. I know that my father still has the same old leather-washer-handled Marble knife that I remember from nearly forty years ago. (I'm sure he got it from a subscription offer connected to a marvelous magazine called *Fur, Fish & Game*, which featured breathtaking stories about trapping by Maurice H. Decker.)

You can imagine how much I wanted a knife that I could carry on my belt as I walked my trapline or rumbled around with my dogs and how equally impossible the whole thing seemed when patches were patched and it was often a problem just to change the cardboard in our shoes about every other day. (I did have a half-ax my grandfather gave me, but now I'm not sure if it was really a half-ax or just what remained from what was once a whole ax with a sawed-off handle.)

Along with the pocketknife discarded by the elders, most of us had one or two others—also discarded, but usually with one blade that had been broken. These knives were relegated to the fishing-tackle box or put away for reasons I don't remember and saved with the other boyhood treasures, like good shooting marbles, in a wooden cigar box and kept in your room. Once in a while, and not very often, you could trade one of those broken knives off to a less fortunate neighbor, or even less frequently, they were given to your kid brother for doing some chore that you were officially assigned but hated—like keeping the kindling box filled in the kitchen. Or filling the kerosene lamps and washing the glass chimneys. (Remember the old galvanized gallon kerosene can? The little cap that fit over the spout was always lost immediately and replaced by a half potato.)

Of course my father would never lend me his good knife—
the one he always carried in his pocket—because he knew from
long experience that I would use it for prying out nails from
boards, practice throwing it against the barn siding, and break the
handle or worse. Or that I'd lose it—as I had the last one he gave
me. And things today are still the same. I'm absolutely incapable
of keeping a pocketknife—even though I put one in all my hunting coats and scatter others around in most of my pants, I still can
never come up with one when I really need it. They just seem to
disappear from me. And Pop still, in his infinite knowledge of
whom he's dealing with, won't let me borrow his. But Someone,
in his infinite sense of mercy, has seen fit to see to it that I get a
second chance. The old Marble sheath knife I so dearly coveted
years ago is still not to be trusted to me, but now I finally got
even—and a little better! Through a series of fortunate circumstances I have become the owner of a magnificent trio of belt
knives. One by Loveless, one by Corbett Sigmund and a Morseth sent to me by A. G. Russell. No grown-up kid ever appre-
ciated anything more than the day last fall when I was out in the
garden patch with my father cleaning ducks. I asked him to let
me borrow his knife and he, predictably, turned me down and offered to do the cleaning job himself instead.

I stopped him in the middle of his speech about my care-
lessness (I could repeat it from memory since I was twelve) and
said that I thought I really did have my own knife in my hunting
coat and laid out the Loveless, the Morseth and the Sigmund and
began using them—each in turn—on the ducks. I waited a while
for him to say something and finally he asked, "Somebody give
you the knives?" "That's right," I said. He continued working
on his duck and thinking of the ultimate fate of those beautiful
knives I had laid out on the log. He simply said, "Son, they don't
know you like I know you."

Well, he's right. Bob Loveless and Corbett Sigmund and A.

G. Russell don't really know me. But I'm not going to use their knives on nails because I'm too lazy or busy to go up to the barn for a claw hammer. I don't have anybody to play mumblety-peg with any more and I know I'll never get the knack of sticking a knife in a barn board from five or six feet away. I may not learn fast—but I eventually learn something. So I intend to take the best care I know of the knives I've got. And I'll use them all—except one. Way in the back of a drawer is an old worn-out dollar-fifty Barlow, the skinning blade down to the nub and the horn handles polished yellow and smooth from years of trapping and farm work. Pop said, some time ago, that he wasn't ever going to give me another knife if I lost that one. And I can promise you one thing—I never, never will.

THE WATERBUCK

STANDING IN the high grass and covered by the shadows of an acacia, the smoke-gray hide of the waterbuck was barely visible through the 4X scope. I would track the cross-hairs down and back from his horns and time and again not be able to be sure of where I had to shoot. I felt, rather than saw, that he also stood with his body curved like a C, but I couldn't tell exactly which way—toward me or not.

When I finally did shoot it was more from desperation than surety, and the animal paused for a second and then ran away into heavier cover before I could work the bolt to shoot again.

The guide asked me where I thought I'd hit him and I said I really wasn't sure I'd hit him at all; but one of the trackers, to my dismay, said he'd heard the bullet strike. When we reached the shadowed spot where the buck had stood we found two or three small spits of blood, then nothing more except trodden grass where he'd knifed his way into heavier cover.

As we quartered the area back and forth trying to find his trail again I kept trying to remember what I had seen through the scope, and the more I thought about it the more convinced I was that my shot was uncallable; that it was hurried, careless and inexcusable. And, with a small sense of relief, I also felt that it had probably been ineffectual. I was sure that I had held too high because of the heavy grass and the darkness of the bush—which tends to make distances seem more than they really are. I started to say that I was sure I had held too high and merely creased the neck, when we found another very small, but very real, drop of blood on a stalk of grass.

I was more than ever convinced that the hit was very superficial, but as we all know you can never be sure. I'd taken too many animals that never bled at all to ever be positive about these things.

Following the tracker was slow and painstaking. Every bush, every stone—every conceivable search for sign had to be made before another step could be taken. And just as we were about to agree that the trail had disappeared—another drop of blood would lead us on. Watching the tracker only served to increase my sense of futility, and my only real contribution now was to keep my rifle ready and watch as far ahead as I could on the rare chance that the buck would suddenly jump up ahead of me.

And then, with no more warning than an instant of a cooling breeze, we were in a torrential rain. A ten-minute downpour that left the African clay puddled and shiny—and trackless.

On the long, wet walk back to the hunting car the guide and I barely exchanged a word. He was, I assumed, rightly upset with me for missing an animal that we'd been looking for for days. He didn't know that I'd had such difficulty seeing the buck through the scope—nor did he know that now I was thoroughly convinced that I shouldn't have shot at all, that I knew too well that I should have waited until conditions changed.

At the car, I unloaded my rifle and cased it for the ride back to camp. My hunter began to chat about what we would do tomorrow, and it seemed as if the incident of the afternoon was passed over to be forgotten as one of those things that happen on a hunt: he had found the animal . . . and I had rather botched it. And that, as far as he was concerned, was the end of it. But it wasn't the end of it for me. Because while we had been making the stalk and later while we were working the sparse blood trail something in my subconscious had been working, and now, after time to dwell on it, I had finally and honestly realized what had happened. And why.

The waterbuck is not a very rare or very difficult animal to find in East Africa, but for one reason or another we hadn't been able to find a decent head for several days even in country where waterbuck are frequently in good number. In fact, I'd more or less given up my hopes of finding one. So when we spotted the big, gray male I shot at, it had come as rather a surprise to all of us and I had that odd feeling that this was an animal I somehow didn't deserve and it became, however subconsciously, an animal that I really was not prepared to take. Remembering how long I fussed over the shot, I was now sure that it was partly the difficulty of it—but a difficulty that gave me time to make half a wish that the smoky shape would take that one or two more steps behind the trees and fade unseen into the bush. My reasons for feeling this way are, to say the least, complicated and personal. But I deeply believe that the same emotions have been shared by all of us. Sometimes we heed them. Sometimes not.

Isn't there a time or two you can remember when somehow an animal you've hunted has done something to make you let him vanish in the woods? Isn't there a bass in a certain spot that somehow you always manage to approach a bit badly? Isn't there a bird or covey that somehow always manages to catch you with your gun on safe—even when you know it's there?

I think we all know times that for almost certain we gave the hunt to the quarry.

We are all aware that there are certain animals and birds and fish that under certain circumstances or in certain places we just refuse to kill. We have somehow given this game, at this place, at this time, a different identity; it has, for whatever reason, come to mean more to us than just another head of game.

We even do the same thing, more or less, among ourselves in competition. Haven't you seen a good shot lose a match to a man not his equal? Don't you know people who just don't want the title of "champion"? Or who couldn't live with the idea of being "best"?

What would our lives be like if we never missed a shot? I think most of us need a day, or a trip or a season—or even a life-time—to be a little short in its successes. I think most of us feel a touch of needed humanity about ourselves in our imperfections—and find great comfort in the times when we are much less than perfect or much less than good enough.

SELF-IMPROVEMENT

FOR SOME REASON or other, there's been a lot of recent publicity about cosmetic surgery for men. Not that my face has such splendid contours that it couldn't use a helping hand here and there, but the idea of this sort of pruning and landscaping just never had much appeal to me. I keep seeing these advertisements in print, however, and finally it dawned on me that there might be a really practical application for cosmetic surgery other than to make basic repairs.

Furthermore, I stand second only to one man I know in being completely and totally committed to avoiding any medical hanky-panky with my epidermal envelope. The lengths to which I am prepared to go to avoid any cutting for any reason—except for one—are unparalleled.

I *could* be talked into something that would improve my trap and skeet shooting. I imagine that something could be done surgically about the problem of lifting my head and shooting over so many targets. A tuck or so in a muscle here or there might just turn the trick. I'm a bit stoop-shouldered anyway and I doubt that anyone would ever notice the difference. There is, I'm sure, a surgeon who could design me around a gunstock, since doing it the other way around hasn't been very effective.

A friend of mine was advised by his psychiatrist to give up trap and buy a bulldozer to relieve his tensions. I think that's taking the easy way out—financially as well as emotionally. I don't see why a few hours spent with an understanding surgeon couldn't give me the classic stance of Dan Orlich. And while the good doctor is at it, he might figure out a way to remove some of the oversize gluteus I carry around and move it up north a couple of feet to strengthen my arms and offer me a permanent recoil pad.

I'm fully convinced that the idea bears merit. Every day we read about some athlete or other having this or that patched or welded or braced so he can continue to make his living. Why not patch or weld or brace me so I can continue to shoot without losing the money I make elsewhere? I'm sure I could find men of the cloth as well as eminent sociologists who would support the logic of my argument. If the Dallas Cowboys and the Baltimore Orioles have a raft of attending specialists, why not employ physicians to minister to the members of Pine Valley Gun Club? Doctors ought to hang around gun clubs more anyway. I've never yet heard a man step up to shoot who said he wasn't feeling poorly. Stand behind two men who are ready to meet each other in a shoot-off and listen to them compare symptoms. It makes you wish you were a mortician. It must have been a trapshooter who said, "I've never beaten a well man yet!"

I ought to draw up a list of things I want done and put it out for bids. I could use a better bearing or something for my left knee so I could pivot. Same goes for the right knee. The doc should do something with nerves to cure flinch. He could shorten my right arm, lengthen my left arm, increase the sensitivity of my trigger finger.

I can close my eyes and see it now. I'm standing on Station Five at the gun club. Behind me are a group of stern-faced men in long white coats with stethoscopes in their pockets. I put my trap gun to my shoulder and call "Pull." A vicious right-angle target screams out and I pivot fluidly, my head locked to the stock, and the target becomes a puff of smoke. Another and another follow, and I am deadly. I do the same thing on left angles from Station One, and the stern faces begin to smile and nod approvingly to each other. I step back to the 27-yard line and one doctor, a shooter himself, stands beside me, and as I run an easy 25 straight, a tear forms in his eye. He is smiling at my wife and children, who have also been watching, and they're smiling too—for the first time since I took up trap . . . or trap took up me.

TOMORROW'S

I GUESS EVERYBODY has a way of assuring himself that tomorrow will, indeed, bring better things. More prudent men save their money, practice on low house 8, or refuse to postpone until tomorrow what they know they should do today. I plan trips. Furthermore I plan them in detail, trips that I know I'll probably never even come close to making.

For example, I'm trying to locate a fairly inexpensive .375 magnum and I am planning a place around home to shoot it every now and then on the theory that someday I'll hunt the greater kudu and the giant sable. There's an empty place in my gun rack (there are a lot of empty, but reserved, places in my gun rack) for the .375, right next to my .338 Winchester magnum that I acquired many years ago on the slim premise that I might someday hunt the huge brown bear. Sitting next to the .338 is a Model

70 .270 sighted in for 250 yards, in case I ever get a chance at bighorn sheep. Below the rifles is a skinning knife, pristine, except that now and then I take it out and run the blade across a stone and shave a hair or so off my arm to prove beyond a doubt to me that should the chance arise, I'm ready. Across the room are maps of Africa, British Columbia and Alaska.

A very experienced hunter once told me that, to him, the hunt was over when he had the quarry in the cross-hairs of the scope. To me, the hunt begins with the unfolding of a map. It may be an evening reverie over a quail hunt in South Carolina or the dream of stalking something in Tanzania.

I have brochures that tell me what to pack and wear in East Africa. I have maps with red lines drawn on them that tell me how to get from home to the places where the wild turkeys live. And when I chance to meet a guide from the South who promises me a fine shoot over good dogs should I ever get a chance to be down his way, I thank him, and we make a mutually mythical date to hunt together.

And now and then, I really go, not as far or as fancily as I can go by leafing through my brochures, but at least enough to taste a different flavor of the wind. That's one of the great things about hunting—there's always someplace else to go and something else to see. One dream fuels another, reassuring us of a reason for being. Right this minute there's a campfire burning somewhere, and I can smell the smoke. Somewhere there's an old bull elk that I might meet, a pointer that I might shoot over or a lion that I will listen to at night.

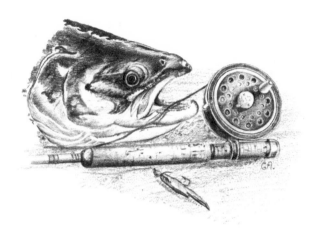

FISHING STRONGER WATERS

SOME YEARS AGO a major magazine published a cartoon showing two ardent outdoorsmen in a boat. One was saying, as he uncorked a bottle, "Beer's all right for trout, but for pike and bass—give me a nice, light ale!"

My first reaction was a laugh. My second—the feeling we've all shared—was that there is great truth in humor. The only thing "dry" about most fishing is a certain type of artificial lure. So I believe that we should make a study of what is the most appropriate beverage to imbibe while angling for certain species of fish.

The problem is not simple for the reason that there are more types of fish than types of alcoholic refreshments. We must, therefore, categorize according to the size of the fish sought, where it's taken (stream, lake, ocean, river and so on) and the general climatic conditions that prevail. We will attempt to

67

equate the sporting qualities of the fish and its locale with common and necessary tonic beverages.

Let me begin by saying that I don't think beer (or ale) should enter into it. There should *always* be beer, unless the temperature, such as often occurs while ice fishing, is below the freezing point. Beer is as necessary for giant tuna as it is to the quiet worm-dunker, half-asleep in the sun, hoping, not very hard, to pick up a few crappies to prove to his wife that he really was fishing for the good of the family larder, not just out to have a splendid time by himself—an attitude all women violently oppose.

Nor are we discussing what you should have back at the camp or the cabin or stuck off somewhere in the boat. We are referring to the niceties of liquid refreshment that a man can and should carry on his person or as part of his regular equipment. In short, gentlemen, we speak of that noble instrument THE FLASK. For those who are needy of potions requiring a high or low temperature, we will later propound the advantages of the "short Thermos."

The flask should carry your initials and those of your next of kin in case of accident—or worse, loss of the flask. If you favor spinning tackle, trolling equipment or any sort of inexpensive glass rod, the modern (and unbreakable) polyethylene flask is good enough. If you are a purist favoring dry flies, Orvis rods and multi-pocketed tailored wading jackets, you are in a position that necessitates the carrying of a nickel, silver or pewter container.

If you favor bass plugging after dark, your flask should have a luminous paint finish and some kind of flotation should it be dropped overboard. If you are a "still fisherman" of the 25¢ bamboo-pole-and-string variety, I'm sure you have long since chosen the proper Mason jar, and have carefully protected it with several wrappings of friction tape.

As you can see, I am making the tacit recommendation that you have a "wardrobe" of flasks so that you may suit the flask to the fishing. There is nothing more distastefully showy than a man deep-trolling with a hand line (probably with a live frog and a June bug spinner) and flashing an engraved silver warmer.

Almost as bad, but not quite, is a correspondent of mine, one E. Schwiebert of New Jersey, who so favors handmade bamboo rods of the ounce-and-a-half persuasion that his flask has been veneered with simulated wickerwork and tasseled in the basic colors of a Royal Coachman. One affectation is as bad as the other.

Another bad example of the showy is a wealthy playboy, E.Z. of Scarsdale, who has had made at considerable expense, hand-fitted flask covers in various plaids to match a variety of fishing shirts.

But, as important as the flask is, it must remain secondary to the selection of what fills it. This may be best explained by example: If I were, for illustration, fishing for salmon in Norway I would carry a silver flask filled with aquavit. Or on the Miramichee in New Brunswick, a pewter flask brimming with an eight-year-old Canadian rye. Another: smallmouths in the Rangeley Lakes of Maine (using a 5½-foot plug rod of bamboo) require a gallon jug of 1959 hard cider.

See how simple it is when given a little thought? But it can get tricky. Imagine being invited to try a private beat for salmon in northern Britain. You guess a fine dry sherry? Wrong. Here it depends on the size of the fish. Sherry is fine for trout, but for grilse you must stay with an 86-proof scotch.

In America, it's really simple, disregarding the local exceptions that we cannot go into here. For stream fishing (I assume for trout) we like to stay with applejack, or scotch if you're east of the Mississippi River (with the exception of Pennsylvania, where it is preferred to offer rye).

When lake fishing—and we can pretty much disregard the size of the fish since the majority of fishermen do likewise—I like to stay with brandy when the weather's cold and favor a red wine when summer comes.

Speaking of hot and cold brings us to the vacuum bottle. Again it isn't too difficult for our common sense to see us through: whiskey sours, john collins and toddies when the weather is chilly or we are on the lake. For warm-weather or stream fishing, gin slings, rum and tonic or a nicely chilled white wine and soda will see us through without disgrace; these also do very nicely on salt water, and are especially well received amid a nice run of blues or fluke.

This, gentlemen, I consider just a basic primer and it is done in answer to many requests. Local options make really sweeping generalizations impossible. If, for example, you plan a sturgeon jaunt along the Snake, or a week afloat on the Arkansas, I will answer you according to your specific needs.

You may have noticed I have neglected to mention the martini. One cannot really limit the use of the martini or presume to dictate when or where it cannot be taken. I once advised a Mr. Cornelius Ryan to carry his martinis (without which he would not fish) in a hot-water bottle since he is a notoriously poor wader and we feared either breakage or loss from a fall. This has proved extremely successful since most of his companions now think he is slightly arthritic and don't let him cut camp wood, cook or dig the latrine. Moreover, he can carry it into his sleeping bag without arousing undue comment.

HOW TO CHEW TOBACCO

A LOT OF THINGS in my life strike a lot of people as foolish—if not downright shameful—such as being seen in the company of known skeet shooters and dry-fly fishermen. But in the last year I have managed to achieve a new low, according to many of my social acquaintances, or more exactly, ex-social acquaintances. Oh hell, I might as well come right out with it: I chew tobacco.

I chew tobacco where nobody else chews tobacco—at fancy dinner parties, during cocktail hours, at business meetings and on bairplanes. I chew because I like it, and I expect to continue to chew where I please and when I please. In fact the only problem I have with the whole business is chewing *what* I please.

When I was a younger fellow I could walk into the general store and stand enthralled before an almost-infinite selection of multicolored packages of snuff—both the kind you tucked under

71

your lip and the kind you pinched between your thumb and fore-finger or put on the back of your hand, then snuffed up your nose. There were plugs of chewing tobacco, small, bricklike and efficient-looking. Day's Work, Apple and Honey Cut are the few I remember. The regular chewing tobacco was offered in a multitude of cuts and flavors. I believe the most popular choices were Mechanic's Delight, Mail Pouch, Beechnut and Red Man. The last three I can still find if I do a lot of hunting around.

But as a kid, I was a pipe smoker. The nickel corncob was within economic possibilities for me, and since my mother and father, of course, had forbidden me to smoke, I had them hidden all over: in the hen house and in the barn; in hollow trees along my trapline; and a couple down by the lake where we kept the rowboat. Cigarettes were expensive—about two packs for fifteen cents, although I seem to remember that I could buy them for a penny apiece. I would once in a great while spring for a pack of Twenty Grands or Sunshines, but for day in and day out I stuck with the pipe and a nickel paper of No. 1 or George Washing-ton. I still recall that the nickel papers were strong as a green brush fire, but I must have considered myself a pretty tough fel-low, because I stuck with it. But when I stuck it pretty good on the trapline or put in a day or so of paid work splitting wood for my grandfather, I temporarily moved up to Edgeworth or Model, which were twice as expensive.

I know I tried chewing because a lot of the men I admired chewed, but I just couldn't make a go of it. There was a romance about chewing and spitting in the coal scuttle while yarning around the stove. I wished I could have pulled it off, but I had to be content with whatever small dash I could exhibit by lighting kitchen matches under my thumbnail or on the bottom of my front teeth and by firing up my pipe without showing that I had burned my thumb and that the inside of my mouth tasted of sul-phur. All the while I kept an eye peeled for my mother or father or my kid brother, who was forever squealing on me at home about smoking.

You know how things like that stick with you. And the picture of an old bird-shooter pausing for emphasis while he dipped into his pack of Red Man and filled his cheek, and worked it down to the spot where it felt just right, has over the years taken on an aura that could not be denied.

About a year ago I began sneaking a little Copenhagen snuff when I was out in the field or out fishing or up on the tractor. I liked it all right. I still will dip a little when the mood comes on me, but that still wasn't chewing. Things came to some sort of head when my wife found out that my daughter, who was then attending kindergarten, was sneaking a little snuff in her lunch box. I knew she took a little grain or two when she was with me on the tractor, and I thought it was cute and let it go at that, but my household is not a democracy—I wasn't allowed to vote. Neither was Jennifer.

Anyway, there comes a time in a man's life when he's got to have the courage to stand up to his wife and daughters, however awesome that confrontation can become, and however mightily he would wish it were otherwise, so I got hold of some Pay Car and started in. Now it's one thing to want to chew, and it's another thing to do it. You have to learn how—and I went at it solo. You learn first off that chewing is a misnomer. You don't *chew*; you just take an amount, which you determine by your personal physical make-up, tuck it in your face between the gum and the cheek and more or less leave it alone.

Right off, let me tell you that you don't ever need a spittoon, if you calculate the amount right. If you're in a duck blind and want to test yourself against an incoming wind, you can enjoy the skills of expectoration, but you don't absolutely have to spend your day watering the area around you.

Time passed, and the more I chewed, the more I liked it, but

I knew something was amiss: there was a void in this new sport, and that was variety. It's hard enough where I live to get chewing tobacco at all, and to have the freedom of choice among flavors, cuts and strengths that the men of my youth enjoyed was no longer possible. Or so I thought, until a friend of mine, as a joke, brought back for me, from a trip down South, a package filled with exotic stuff: several plugs like Bloodhound, Brown Mule, Black Maria and Bull of the Woods; and a few papers of chewing tobacco called Red Fox. The package itself was a work of art, and as I tucked away a modest amount, I felt delight that must have been near to what Pierre Pérignon felt when he first tasted champagne. You've heard that every man deserves to have one good gun and one good dog. I add to that one perfect chewing tobacco.

It didn't take too long until I'd gone through what he'd brought me, and it took less time to discover that no one, absolutely no one, for what appeared to be a hundred miles around, sold it. It seemed that I had but just discovered the *ne plus ultra* of chews only to realize that I might as well have only dreamed it.

I happened to wistfully mention my lost love to a close neighbor, Tom Young, whom I knew hailed from South Carolina, and whom I knew for a fact was returning there to visit his family. Before too long, Tom had promised to strip the state of Red Fox and that after his return I would never want again. Tom left on his trip, and after a week or so I began to scan his driveway, hoping to see his car. Then I'd think that maybe he'd forgotten anyway, and I'd console myself with something else.

I'd about given up on Tom when late one night, he knocked on my door and handed me a paper bag with a note on it. He left saying he'd just that minute gotten home and had to go back and help his wife get the luggage out of the car. I shook open the bag and a dozen packages of Red Fox fell on the kitchen table. I couldn't get a handful quick enough! When I was contentedly rolling an ounce or so from one jaw to the other, I picked up Tom's note and read it: "My grandfather, who has been in the business, told me that the secret of good tobacco was not altogether in the leaf. He said that one had to take a mind to how it's cured. Some folk stoke up their fires too fast and they burn it right up. And others are so afraid of burning it that they let their barn get too cold, and it cures green. Good tobacco has to be properly dried, then cured and finally fixed at successively higher temperatures.

"Nowadays, when one is forced to cross the country in a few hours and drink three-day-old beer, ain't it a pleasure to know, as I'm sure you do, that good friends, good bourbon and good tobacco are slowly made."

THE HAPPY WIFE

IN THE OLD DAYS, the wife of a hunter was kept involved with his fortunes a good deal more than is true today. When a man went forth with his matched pair of spears (probably the equivalent of improved cylinder for short throws and full choke for the longer) and returned in his own good time, his wife got down to the chores of skinning, cutting up the meat, and discussing with him the advantages of twenty-four-lines-per-inch checkering on the spear shaft as opposed to eighteen or twenty. She was interested in how he felt about the balance of his clubs, axes and the like, and clung to his every word as she patiently chewed the skins to the suppleness of his liking.

The nostalgic beauty of such a tranquil scene is, of course, almost irrevocably lost to us. You arrive home tired, thirsty and eager to tell the Queen Bee what a helluva fellow she was lucky enough to garner when you're reminded that she has spent all day waxing and polishing the floor. If you make a feeble joke about "At least the mop handle has a nice piece of wood even if it seems to be a trifle butt-heavy," you may be accused of having spent most of the day at Mario's Cherry Croft Inn.

I think she tends to stay apart from the long, detailed conversations about choke boring and the perilous indecision you might someday have to conquer in the selection of sidelocks over box-locks because she lacks the involvement of her ancestors. Simply, we have been too selfish.

I have made a point (never mind the obvious self-sacrifice) of not only permitting but encouraging my wife to pick and clean every bird I bring home. Never mind that the local poultry shop in Easton, Maryland, will do the complete job on my Canada geese for a dollar or so—I bring mine home *en plumage*. I'm sure that part of the deep pleasure my wife exhibits in serving rabbit stew is the fact that I bought her a nice light skinning knife for her last birthday and taught her how to use it.

Right now I'm partway finished on a project that will bring tears to her eyes: a custom-made linoleum kitchen flooring designed to resemble exactly the muddy footprints of English setters, Labrador retrievers and the sole prints of my Gokey and Bass boots and my insulated waders—so real that you'd believe we'd all just stepped out of the swamp.

This, when completed, should obviate the necessity of mopping and waxing the floor forever and release her so she can spend more time reloading my trap shells for me, keeping my field clothes mended and boning up my boots with Sno-Pruf. In the winter evenings before the fire she takes great delight in carefully cleaning the checkering on my shotguns and palming warm linseed oil into the stocks while I read her tidbits from Thomas's *Shotgun Lore for the Sportsman,* or advice from Churchill on wing shooting. For a special treat, I recall exactly for her every decent score I've ever made on trap or skeet, with special emphasis on the misfortunes beyond my control that caused the occasional miss.

Rest assured that I am doing everything in my power to convince the management of outdoor magazines to include a woman's editor, creating a special section for our wives. There'll be patterns so they can make our hunting clothes for us, exercises to strengthen their wrists so they can work a handtrap to help us sharpen our shooting eye, and the like.

An example of what ingenuity women can achieve when they're on the right track is the discovery my wife made when she was testing the performance of some 7½s she had loaded for my trap gun. From 40 yards they'll penetrate to page 203 of Kate Millet's book, *Sexual Politics.*

SANCTUARY

WHAT'S THE SPECIAL feeling that you have about a piece of wa-ter—a brook, a spring, a river, a pond or lake? Why is it that the real outdoorsman instinctively checks his step and approaches such a place as he would approach a church? I think in part it's because we hesitate to break the quiet that usually surrounds a pond.

That's some of it at least—but more than merely awe of quiet is the feeling that we really don't belong. A shoreline is a foreign place to man. A shoreline, even of a tiny spring, belongs to the heron poised above a napping frog, a working muskrat, a feeding fish or, best of all, a deer staring at its own upside-down, sky-framed reflection.

The edge of water is a place of surprise to man—a place of sanctuary to the wild. A waterhole is usually a place of truce

79

where the preying and the preyed-upon can live side by side in peace.

I never really understood my own small pond in just quite that way until a day last fall when, sneaking past the willow tree, I heard the soft, contented feeding chatter of a pair of ducks that had slipped in as silently as sifting leaves. As I watched these hefty, merry canvasbacks I became aware of a shifting of emotions deep within myself.

Had I had a gun, and had I seen this pair come weaving through the trees in flight, I have no doubt that I'd have shot and considered myself lucky at the chance. But that's not what I felt at all, now that they were sitting feeding at a table in my house. No longer were they wild ducks—abstract fragments in the sky— now they were suddenly *particular* ducks, *my* ducks. A hen and drake, hungry, and obviously very pleased to be exactly what they were. They had sanctuary.

So is it with the deer that feed on fallen apples from the greenings and the northern spies that line my lane. They are not abstract but particular deer. My deer.

I've come home from woodcock covers empty-handed more than once to find a flight down in the birches by the brook, but by being there, in my "backyard," they become particular and not abstract. My woodcock, my "house covey."

What greater satisfaction can there be to you than knowing you are man enough to know when not to shoot and why; having the understanding of sanctuary, the ability to separate the abstract from the particular?

Who should better know the importance of sanctuary than we who must turn out-of-doors to find it? Yours may be the mountains and mine the valleys with a spring-run brook, but the purpose is the same. To find a spot where we can be at peace, not only with ourselves, but just as important, away from others. A place where we can find our identity . . . become particular men, not abstract beings. As the deer feed on apples and the ducks forage through the pond, we are no less seeking food—just sustenance in a different form. A tasting of the wind. A feeding of the mind on quiet. A place to place ourselves, to simply rest our minds; to bank the fires of ambition.

To understand the meaning of sanctuary is to understand one of the earliest concepts of man.

The concept of sanctuary extends beyond place into circumstance as well. For example, I have a friend who is as fine a wing-shot as I have ever seen, and his bird dogs are as good at their role in the field as he is at his. After seeing him return again and again with only one bird or, on rare occasions, two, I just had to ask him why a man with his ability with a shotgun and teamed up with dogs the like of his came back with so little to show for it. "I've discovered my own way of 'throwing them back,' " he said.

"Instead of using barbless hooks I use a kind of shell-less gun. The dogs get the same amount of work—I even find it easier to handle them when they need it now that I don't shoot. But shooting doesn't prove anything to me any more. I let the dogs do their work. I flush the bird, swing through it with my gun and watch it fly away. I only shoot what I want to eat." He handed me a couple of blank field-trial shells and winked at me.

I know we all understand sanctuary in our private way and have come, through experience and conscience, to know that we must first give it to others in order to have the comfort of it for ourselves.

A TRAPSHOOTER'S CONFESSION

No POET will ever dedicate a lyric to the clay target, and I'm afraid that my trapshooting is as bad as my verse—or worse—but how I love the game! I grew up in that long-lost era where children were seen and not heard. No right-thinking parent, surely not mine, ever deviated from the proven principle of "spare the rod and spoil the child," and they weren't much worried about our growing up maladjusted, either. So my introduction to clay-target shooting was working the trap and collecting the unbroken targets. No one ever considered letting me shoot. I never considered asking.

How I envied the shooters back in those days. The cool skill they exhibited with the single-barrel Foxes, Parkers and Ithacas seemed to me to be the absolute epitome of grandeur. I know that I was a terrible wing shot myself, and I'm sure that was no little part of my awe.

A TRAPSHOOTER'S CONFESSION

One of the nicest things about old gun clubs is the row after row of sepia-colored photographs of the gunners in their buttoned-at-the-collar work shirts, the careful hair combs above the starched collars framing a serious set to the eyes that could seemingly shatter targets with a glance. (There's a picture of me and George Coe and Ken Gibson taken a year ago at a shoot and we all have our hats on sideways and look rather silly; it seems a mockery of the days when men were more serious about their shooting pastimes. Of course, we don't shoot as well, either.)

I shot my first trap at the kind of shoots that country gun clubs arrange to earn money. You paid fifty cents or a dollar and shot at ten targets. The prize was a chicken. (I seem to remember a preponderance of leather-skinned Rhode Island Reds. Somehow it always seemed fitting to shoot for something you could eat.) I don't think I ever shot ten straight—if anyone did he walked pretty tall and was whispered about at all the other shoots for the entire fall.

The trap was set up behind hay bales and scrap lumber and you could count on some pretty wild targets. No matter how badly you shot there was always some old buddy who'd say, "Well, mebbe he can't hit them clay targets, but byjeezus you ought to see him when it's got feathers on it!" (If anybody said that about me, it was likely me.)

If you showed up with a single-barrel or a Model 12 Winchester everybody talked about the "regular trap gun," no matter what it really was. The most common guns were the old side-by-sides: Lefevers, Trojan- and Vulcan-grade Parkers, Model 24 Winchesters and the bottom-of-the-line LCs and Ithacas. They all had double triggers, extractors and thirty-inch barrels and were sworn to be all full choke. And more than one was wired and taped together. Most of them kicked like hammers.

The shoots always had a "dead mark." You bought a square inch marked out on the back of an old movie poster with X in it from corner to corner. Someone shot at it, and the person whose square had the shot closest to the cross of the X won a turkey.

The ladies brought food, mostly cakes and pies, sold coffee and soda and flirted with the men to get them to buy chances on the dead mark or to shoot another round of trap.

I found a shoot like that again last fall and foolishly turned up in my shooting jacket, with my two pair of shooting glasses. Although I knew one or two farmers there casually, I'm afraid I was the center of all eyes as I uncased my trap gun. I was very well aware that I was almost the only man there with a real trap jacket and a real trap gun. Everybody else had on their work clothes and brought the gun they shot everything with. I paid my dollar and stepped up to the line. The trap was some kind of old, hand-fed job and threw the targets almost straight up in the air.

I knew they'd be hellishly hard to hit and was overwhelmed when I smoked the first five, six and seven. Everybody else had missed one or two—and then I dropped three in a row. The winner had broken eight. "No smartass with his special gun and clothes is gonna come here and show us how to shoot," was the relieved general attitude when I walked off the line. I knew how I used to feel not too long ago and I must admit I agreed with them. It wouldn't have been fitting or right if I'd won.

I think my first registered trap shoot happened to be at the Grand American at Vandalia, Ohio—the Olympics of trapshooting. I just happened to be there and decided I wanted to shoot, so I borrowed a gun and shot. Mercifully, I've forgotten my score. But I do remember leaving with the firm belief that nobody is born that bad a shot, and with the firm conviction that I could learn if I only had my own trap gun. So shortly after that I became the owner of an old nickel-steel Model 12. And, hat in hand, I turned up at a trap club I'd heard about and asked if I could shoot.

Like most trap clubs they couldn't have been more pleasant. I was even invited back—mostly because trapshooters are as full of advice as golfers and delight in finding a head as empty as mine that they can fill with advice and theories.

The terrible transition from a normal human being into a trapshooter is hell on a man's family. First off, you decide that the reason everybody shoots better than you do is that they have more odds and ends of equipment: shooting glasses, shooting gloves, shooting hats, shell cases, eyeshades. All this is acquired in a great rush so you, too, can become an expert. I had my Model 12 restocked. I added a trigger shoe. I tuned the trigger. I still fumbled.

The answer was obvious: more guns. Guns came and went in graduated economic progression. The checkering became finer, the engraving more profuse—the scores stayed the same. No fortune seemed more fickle and alluring than 50 straight—or none seemingly less attainable. But at least I had finally gotten to the point where there were worse shooters. Not many, but some.

My bedside table was (and still is) littered with printed advice: Lee Braun's book on trap, Fred Missildine's book on trap, books on choke boring, books on wing shooting, Captain Bogardus and Purdey and Churchill and Etchen. Books that say hold a low gun, books that say hold the gun high. I've tried swinging through, pointing out and towing targets—in short, I know everything about the game. Too much, I guess, because I can never settle down and stick with one routine. I'm ⅓ Etchen, ⅓ Braun and ⅓ Missildine. And I guess the parts don't really fit together.

One of the alluring things about trap is that it's pretty much the same game of skill no matter what the degree of formality. You can fire above the straightaway and behind the right angles just as easily at the local volunteer fire department shoot as you can at Travers Island. And you can always find somebody better than you are on a given day, anyplace.

The thing that really intrigues me about trap is the endless variety of the shotguns. You can watch a squad take its place on the 16-yard line and see five different guns. The trapshooter never lived who doesn't believe that somewhere there is a trap gun that will solve his problems—and he'll never own it. This is the game for dreamers. With every box of fresh shells comes the idea that this may be the round when I really discover the secret, the little thing that a Dan Orlich knows that I don't . . . yet.

That's the nagging and elusive thing about trap, the so-near-but-yet-so-far mystery of the game. After all, it's not a question of strength or stamina or speed. It's not a question of being fat or thin or tall or short. Or even a man or a woman. Or young or old. If you can break five in a row why can't you break 25? If you can break 25 why can't you continue through 100, and then 200? That's why we keep coming back.

I like trapshooters. I like the talk that floats around a gun club. I'll always feel a little tingle of excitement as I get ready to call for my first bird—and the pleased surprise when I break it. This is about the only sport I know where the winner is usually more embarrassed than the loser, and offers as many excuses.

Trap has given me some of the most pleasant times and some of my closest friends. And that's what it's all about.

I forgot who was remarking about the laws of compensation and went on to say ". . . even take ice, for example, the poor gets theirs in the winter and the rich gets theirs in the summer." I have a wife and two daughters, and trapshooting's made me conveniently hard of hearing. You couldn't say that about golf! (I just remembered who said the bit about ice: Bat Masterson.)

FIRESIDES

"Let's go sit by the fire."

Pick any fire. Any friend. Any place. I'm sure you can think of quite a few fires you'd like to sit by again this minute, reliving a special day that time will never tarnish. Some of the companions may be gone, but shared fires are still remembered as being as bright and warm as friendship.

There are merry fires and fires that invite contemplation. But they all draw men together as does no other shared experience in all the out-of-doors. I guess that for me at least, the huge roaring blazers we built along the shore when fishing through the ice were as happy as any. A big chunk of hardwood formed a backlog and in front was just about anything that would burn—except stuff that was pitchy, because someone was always cooking something just about all day long. There were carefully constructed

87

brush "clotheslines" that could dry a succession of wet mittens, and now and then socks, when we disobeyed our elders and went fooling around the thin ice at the edge of the lake or the spring runs in spite of being told not to.

Another unforgettable fire is the first one you ever built all alone. Mine was on a huge flat rock in the middle of a stream that I'd tempted once too often when fishing for spring suckers and perch. That was the day I sort of had to smile to myself about all the kidding I'd gotten about always carrying my little waterproof match safe—but if you stopped me in the woods tomorrow, or made me rummage down deep in my tackle box, I'd be willing to bet I could come up with dry matches.

I like the small work that goes with a fire and using the old tools that go with it. The careful splitting of thin slivers of kindling, the quartering of logs for next-size-up wood, and working with a hammer and wedges to split reluctant trunks. I guess we all pride ourselves on our prowess at cutting wood and fire building—but I remember too clearly the few times I failed.

One of these failures was back up in a high-country elk camp, and the enemy was a sheetmetal sheepherder's stove. Tucked away in the corner of a tent, it just sat there and mocked me. No matter what I did, I couldn't get the thing to burn for more than fifteen minutes at a time. We sliced kindling so delicate you could have knitted with it, then ever so carefully added inch-square pieces of aspen, and everything would seem to be fine until we left the tent for supper. When we came back, it would all be burned out or just sitting there cold. Even in the few minutes that it seemed to cooperate, it threw out as much smoke as it did heat, so we opted to freeze rather than smother and spent most of our time in the big kitchen tent exchanging lies with the outfitter and getting in the way of the cook.

I like the little five-minute fires an Indian guide used to make when we decided to quit fishing for a while and have tea. Just a couple of stones, a handful of match-size twigs and by the time I'd dipped the kettle in the lake for water, we'd have a little hand-warmer going; in the time it took to make a couple of casts from the shoreline, we'd have tea. Tea just doesn't taste the same any-where else either. Maybe it's the pine-tinted water and the bat-tered tin cup and the quiet—or maybe it's the magic of sharing this blessing with a man with the unlikely name of White Duck—but it's somehow different and less inspiring anywhere else.

I like sitting over a little pail of glowing charcoal in a duck-blind; I know it comforts the eye a lot more than it takes the chill from the bones, but it's a pleasant thing to thaw a trigger finger now and then and be able to disguise a hurriedly made-at-three-a.m. sandwich with a little toasting.

Fire has always been sacred to man; one of the oldest and greatest symbols of his superiority over the beasts. We burned fires at the mouths of our caves for protection from wolves and saber-toothed tigers. All literature is filled with the stories of how one of the gods of a particular people gave them the gift of fire. Ancient firekeepers were specially selected and often ranked high in the religious echelons of both pagan and civilized times. And today we still carry a feeling about fire that we can't explain. It's a feeling that comes from the depths of our early memories when we were more beasts than men ourselves—a feeling of community, perhaps it is, that gives Liberty a lighted torch and kindles that special feeling we all know all too well when we see the little fires at places like Arlington, that pay perpetual honor to our heroes of the past.

A fire is a symbol of being home—wherever that fire is. A fire is a place where we are welcome and find comfort among our kind.

I can still smell the spicy, pungent acacia-wood smoke from an African campfire. Coming home at night we could see the blaze up on the hillside from miles away in the dark, and we knew that our friends would be there waiting to talk about the day past and the day to come. We'd sit around and stare into the flames one minute and up at the stars that make up the Southern Cross the next. From somewhere, the night carried the voices of hyenas and every so often the bass of a lion or the ascending shrill of a petulant elephant. And then we would all, subconsciously and very discreetly, draw the chairs up a little bit closer to the fire.

After supper, we'd come back and sometimes talk a little and sometimes not. And then to bed. I would lie there and watch the orange glow outside through the canvas tent and listen with an ancient ear to these night things and wonder that such a pretty, sweet-smelling thing as fire really stood between me and that basso profundo coming closer in the night from somewhere on Kilimanjaro.

Our fires warm our spirits as much as our bodies. They dry our cares as well as our wet britches and carry our dreams in the flames.

I know of no more welcome phrase, no better way of saying, "Let's share what we have of life right now," than when a friend says to me, "Let's go sit by the fire."

HOW TO BE WELL DRESSED

My wife is forever hollering at me to do something with my gunning clothes—by which she means that she's sick and tired of having them scattered all over the house shedding feathers and chips of mud and handfuls of seeds and twigs and the odd shell or so. It's not that I'm the neatest person around—I don't claim to be—but I get a great deal of satisfaction from knowing that I've got a hunting coat here and a pair of boots there where I can see them. And, furthermore, I've got the dogs on my side. They like to sleep on my hunting stuff, and how can they do that if everything is always hung up somewhere?

Women don't understand these things: they just see the surface and you come off being sloppy instead of thoughtful and logical. They don't understand that hunting clothes have to be broken in and to acquire a certain character that combines an air of rustic comfort with a certain amount of dash.

They don't understand that a man would just as soon show up naked at a hunting camp as wearing a new set of stuff. I just want my pants patched—not ironed. You can look at a man's hunting clothes and tell right away what kind of a guy he is. You can look at a man's hunting clothes and tell what kind of a day you're in for when you're going gunning with him.

I arrived in Connecticut last fall for a couple of days of grouse hunting with Dick Baldwin, who works for Remington. I was dressed like an illustration from William Harndon Foster's *New England Grouse Shooting*—tweed cap, fairly respectable shirt, reasonably good britches and a relatively new pair of leather-topped rubbers.

I must say I presented a decent picture of the "gentleman shooter." At least I could walk into a bar and they wouldn't lock the cash register. Baldwin, my host, guide and long-time friend, didn't say anything after surveying me from top to toe, but I suspect he was relieved that I wasn't affecting a necktie. (Not that I hadn't considered it.)

Dick, to say the least, was a contrast. He was dressed like an extra in a movie about starving Welsh coal miners. He wore what vaguely was reminiscent of what had once been a sweatshirt under one of those old, inch-thick canvas hunting coats. He had on a pair of hunting pants that, years past, had been faced with something the manufacturer had surely advertised as "indestructible." The manufacturer was wrong.

His twelve-inch rubber boots were laceless and you could see his socks through the cuts. An old New York Yankee baseball hat was pulled down over his eyes. As we piled into the car he remarked, "I go through two or three of these outfits a year in these covers." My heart sank at the thought of what lay in wait for me, and I wasn't the least bit disappointed.

I'm sure you're acquainted with the popular illustrations and the traditional watercolors of New England partridge shooting. In the foreground are the beautiful crimson-and-pumpkin-colored maple trees. Scattered about are thinly bunched birches, and the overall impression is a gentle rolling meadow dotted here and there with tinting trees. So much for the popular conception of grouse covers. Real, Dick-Baldwin-type grouse covers are vast, impenetrable, five-acre-sized clumps of briars, six-inch-thick grape vines and scrub oak. All this is studded with rocks that are too high to step over unless it's a bog swamp with the hummocks placed nine inches farther apart than you can step. Somehow this vegetation and mire is always hunted on a forty-five-degree slant upward. (I don't know how you can hunt for two days and never walk downhill, but Baldwin knows.)

A famous historian once wrote, "Experience gives men the ability to act with foresight." He was absolutely right. Next time my hunting partner shows up dressed anywhere near the way Baldwin does I'm going to reach into the trunk of my car and pull out a cane I now carry for exactly those moments, murmur a few words of apology about my old football knee and limp slowly toward the nearest bar.

PUTTING THINGS AWAY

MY GAME-SHOOTING season ended with all the small rituals that go with what I foolishly call "putting things away." The gunning coats are gone through, and all the miscellaneous knickknacks that hunters somehow accumulate are sorted out: pieces of rope; plastic sandwich bags; papers of pipe tobacco with only a half a bowlful left and saved for who knows what reason; matches that will never light; pocketknives that have needed sharpening for two seasons; pipe cleaners that have turned a strange and deadly-looking shade of brown. The dog whistles are taken out and probed for feathers and then hung up on a dowel covered with an empty red-paper shell. The duck and goose calls are probed for feathers and have the dog hair and tobacco crumbs banged out and hung on a dowel covered with an old blue-paper shell. (You can see right away I have a place for everything!) Gloves that have not seen their mates for almost a year are reunited. Shooting glasses are discovered; the missing cases are tracked down and paired off with their rightful contents. And for the first time in many months the 28-gauge shells are separated from the 16s, and the 16s are separated from the 12s.

I am overcome with an incredible energy. Even the hip boots are taken outside and hosed off, then hung upside down on their proper hangers like olive-drab chimneys. The grand finale with the whole orchestra playing is the cleaning of the guns. Linseed and turpentine are rubbed carefully over the wood. The working parts are hosed down with Hoppe's No. 9 until the whole room is dizzying with the one smell that, more than almost any other, makes me already nostalgic for an autumn that is months and months away.

The closing of the gun-cabinet door and the turning of the lock serve as some kind of *amen* to this little ritual that has come to be as patterned as an ancient Mass. But the dogs who watched me go through the moves of putting things away for years seem completely unconcerned. They accept it for what it is, a small ritual that marks a change of pace—the end of the season being a little kind of sadness for us all. But the old dogs know me too well for them to shed a tear for *auld lang syne*. It'll be a week or two at worst until the whistles are shucked off the red brass-headed peg, and we're off for a romp. The carefully glistened shotguns will bark or roar, all in turn and turn again in the back field over our somewhat inefficient trap. The shooting glasses will begin another long journey away from their rightful cases, and the hip boots will be rechristened with mud and left to stand, tops turned down, in the hall. Gloves will be scattered from coat to coat, and the red and yellow and green and blue and violet shells will again be randomly nestled together like pocketsful of Christmas lights.

So ritual follows ritual, each more similar than different, and "putting away" seems only the start of "taking all the things out," so that the ceremony never really ends. I'm sure that these are the rituals we enjoy so much for themselves that we end up like some witless cleric, forever fumbling around in outdoor trappings and robes, forever celebrating a succession of magical rites that by now we are helpless to avoid. The Irish poet Yeats may have had the likes of us in mind when he asked the question: "How can we know the dancer from the dance?"

Indeed, our rituals have rituals within themselves—the excitement of studying maps, the commitment of buying a license, the beguiling mysteries and promises of catalogs, the discoveries of the new and the recalling of the past. I know for a fact that, to a great deal of the world, our comings and goings are trivial and pathetic. They are a lot of silliness with dogs and guns and such—most of it is not understandable and that which is understandable is frequently seen as a rather pitiable effort to stay with what we can of our youth. Well, so be it.

I don't feel a great need to be understood by the rest of the world and would be happier if it would just leave me alone—alone to enjoy my small pleasures amidst my curious toys. Right now, the call of the mourning dove will stand me in good stead for a daily hymn, and to sit watching a woodcock worming along the brook in the meadow is to witness a miracle that I cannot pretend to understand. And things like these I need as part of my rituals— perhaps they are the sole reason for having rituals at all. What is commonplace to one person is to me in every sense wonderful. I find my own explanation of power and glory in the rainbow flushing of the pheasant, the sweet pipings of a string of ducklings and the magic of puppies.

And, hoping I will never know better, I shall go forth with my acolyte dogs and old friends along the banks of spring runs, under longleaf pines, through the ancient muskiness of swamps, finding what I want and getting what I need from the cathedrals of alder and birches. My whistles and calls will be slung around my neck like ancient beads. My old gunning clothes will serve as robes. My leaking boots and frozen fingers will mortify my flesh and the fragrance of Hoppe's will serve as incense. I will be there to serve and learn among the things, creatures, times and places that, for some little part of my life, have come to make me happy and grateful for what I am. And to prepare myself against the frequent, unnamed sorrows that come to haunt my shallow sleep, I have found that I have places to hide—in a willow thicket with my friends the woodcock or above the clouds and below the moon with my friends the geese.

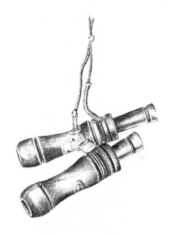

CALLING DUCKS

ULYSSES S. GRANT once remarked that he only knew two tunes. One of them was The Star Spangled Banner and the other one wasn't. And compared to me, General Grant was a musical prodigy. Be that as it may, I am getting my hands on as many duck and goose calls as I can. I intend to learn to call waterfowl even if in the process I offend every ear in the country—and I just might. Even my Labradors have started to slink into the dark recesses of their kennel, and the rest of the world around the farm becomes dumb and silent as I tune up my "highball" and "feeding chatter" out behind the barn.

I thought I had a goose call working pretty good—and I did except the one I had down to an acoustical fine point was the danger call, a single, piercing *honk* that I can reproduce with such fidelity that no goose ever hearing it has stopped climbing until he has reached his maximum altitude, which I believe is somewhere in the neighborhood of 28,000 feet.

My duck calls, on the other hand, are such a curious combination of unnatural sharps and flats that more than one mallard has succumbed and warily circled over my blind, no doubt only out of an incredible aural curiosity rather than what I hoped would be a verbal promise of feathered companionship, great food or a torrid love affair.

Like most of us, I tend to quickly shift any of my own personal shortcomings over to the area of blaming them on faulty equipment and go out and buy something new. Right now I have four different calls, two duck and two geese—and a pintail and widgeon whistle that I won't count, because I haven't gotten around to working on that yet. I'm not sure if anyone makes an instrument that can begin to compensate for the fact that I'm about as tone deaf as a post—but I'm trying them all. And to give myself the pat on the back that I truly deserve, without out-and-out bragging, after only a few months of practice I have come up with a very recognizable version of both "Mary Had a Little Lamb" and "Silent Night" on the harmonica.

There are few things I enjoy more than waterfowling and all that goes with it. The deep envy that I radiate when the weather-tanned guide nonchalantly hauls some birds down within range with a few casual notes on his call is becoming more than I can control. When I'm out behind the barn practicing to the sheep I constantly have this mental image of myself, dressed in hip boots, my old and battered but very distinguished ducking cap pulled just slightly down over my eyes, my three-inch magnum 1100 casually tucked in the crook of my left arm and about four assorted calls strung around my neck. My weather-tanned face warily scans the cold and shallow light of just dawn on a real weather-making morning. My experienced eyes pick out a small flock of ducks—still so far away that the other men in the blind have no idea of their presence.

"Blacks," I say casually. "About two miles off, twelve hundred feet high, at eleven o'clock."

"How can you tell?" ask the greenhorns with me in the blind.

"Count the wingbeats," I whisper, and start to finger the Olt call I favor for distance work.

"He thinks he can call those birds in," followed by not too muffled laughter, comes from behind me in the blind. I turn, silence the chattering with a scowl and put my call to my lips. In spite of the incredible volume, there issues forth a sound so ancient, so pure, so wild, so magically entrancing that even before the lead black starts to turn I can hear the quick snapping as the gunners check the safeties and the rustling of heavy gunning clothes as the men instinctively crouch lower in the blind.

I smile to myself and shift to another call, a gleaming masterpiece made from soft glowing Osage orange. A subtle series of chuckles follows that sounds like a hen mallard reading the menu of a duck's version of the 21 Club. The flock is swiftly closing in and is about to turn upwind and scatter in the blocks. I give the signal for the other guns to stand and take their shots. And after all have missed, I rise and pull a pair of drakes, stone cold, at 55 or 60 yards. Then without a word, I send my perfectly trained retriever into the bay. My weather-tanned face permits itself a slight but manly grin of satisfaction as I turn to the other men and promise that I'll call the next bunch in a little closer—if they'd like. I bring out my pintail whistle and start to work a flock that they have yet to spot, as the Labrador brings in the second duck and puts it in my hand.

So this fall if you should happen to see a weathered ducker in hip boots, a nicely flavored cap pulled down just slightly over his eyes, an automatic magnum tucked in the crease of his left arm, a perfectly mannered Lab at his side and enough calls strung around his neck to make him look like a pipe organ, stop and say "Hello." It's me imitating a duck hunter.

"THE WALLEYE KING"

IF YOU THREATENED to pull out my fingernails with pliers and then strapped me to a lie detector I would probably admit that I like to fish. I, of course, do not associate with dedicated and well-known fishermen for the same reason I do not frolic with anyone featured in the FBI's Most Wanted list. I have enough problems with my own credibility gap being a trapshooter, bird hunter and dog raiser.

So last summer, under a ruse so complicated it would make an excellent theme for a novel on international espionage, I was lured to an isolated lake in Ontario. My companions, being true fishermen, refused to allow me my customary evening stroll beneath the towering pines. They insisted instead that I engage in games of chance with a deck of cards while they breathed their whiskey-laden breath in my face—in spite of my well-publicized aversion to distilled spirits. Their manners paralleled their rude costumes—ill-fitting garments stained beyond all recall with parts of long-expired fish, bug ointments and various malodorous chemicals created to make their strings sink or float.

It seemed I had barely gotten to bed when I was roused, given some food and placed in a boat with the most wretched of the group, a small, dark-haired man whose shifty glance reminded me more of a ferret than anything else. The guide, whose good fortune it was to speak only Algonquin, crouched over the outboard, as much repelled by my companion as I was. After a short run, sufficient to leave me soaked to the skin with freezing spray, the guide made it known that we were to begin fishing.

My companion responded by flinging a huge half-pound spoon within a sixteenth of an inch of my eyebrows and began a litany about "this being the life," while I crouched in a constant state of terror. My partner, proving himself an accomplished fisherman, had contrived a method of casting that left me no area at all to fish except the barren depths on the other side of the boat.

After he had boated three or four undernourished, moronic walleyes, he began a tedious discourse, punctuated by the frequent opening of beer cans, about his legendary way with the walleye. He admitted, reluctantly, that I might, if I wished, refer to him as "the Walleye King." He had been constantly changing my lures for me in an effort to be helpful. I saw it as a transparent device to keep me from catching any fish at all—even though now and then when he ended up with a backlash I managed to throw a plug on the side of the boat that he virtually monopolized. It was valiant, but futile.

As noontime approached the guide indicated that we were to cease fishing and head for lunch on a nearby island. My boatmate (let's call him Jim) responded by finishing the other half of the single beer I had been nursing all morning and, swinging his rod around like a saber, knocked what was left of my pipe tobacco into the bilge.

Lunch itself was uneventful, provided you'd been raised on a farm and were used to the swilling of hogs. After Jim's theft of a number of beers from the other boats he and I started out again and essentially repeated in the afternoon the recreational activities of the morning.

In deference to my younger readers as well as those men and women of normal sensibilities, I will not recount the activities of the evening. As often as I could, I escaped from their rude badinage and stood outside on the porch caught up in the splendor of the summer moon, the fragrance of the evergreens and the mystical enchantment of the voices of the loons. These sounds were contrasted with the voices of my companions, rough-edged with shouting and worse, as they recounted capturing tons of trout, salmon and smallmouth bass under conditions that would have rebuffed a Tartar. The smallest number I heard all night was fourteen—whether it was the weight of an eastern brook trout brought to creel or the point spread on a gin rummy hand, I have no idea.

To say that I faced the coming of the next dawn with mixed emotions would be the understatement of the century. Jim, whom I'd drawn in my boat again, was a good deal more subdued than he'd been the previous day and, except for supervising the loading of half a brewery on my back (to be carried to the boat), he seemed almost tolerable.

The Algonquin stayed in his seat and silently watched as Jim commandeered the best and the softest cushion while I risked a bilateral hernia wrestling the ice chest and its contents into the boat.

After an hour or so I grew more and more uncomfortable from the heat. This was because I had turned the earflaps down on my hat and was wearing a heavy scarf after having bad dreams all the previous night about a set of No. 6 treble hooks sunk deep in an important artery. With that crowd, I felt sure that first aid and last rites would be synonymous, and I wasn't about to rely on luck.

Under the best of circumstances, Jim's coordination was never what you would call outstanding, and today was some sort of a new low. He had one bad backlash after another, and finally got his reel into a mess that looked like it would require a welder's torch to clear up. At last I had a chance to exhibit my deft touch with a casting rod, and my instincts about the correct lures began to pay off. Lunker walleye after lunker walleye was added to the stringer, and now and then a respectable bass. Jim, having given up on his backlash, was reduced to sullenly trolling a June Bug Spinner on the ten or twelve feet of usable line he had left.

At lunch I felt it was my duty to divulge my knowledge of the finer points of casting and of the lifestyle and eating habits of the walleye. That my companions said nothing I took as evidence of their rapt attention. I further insisted on constantly referring to Jim as "the Walleye King" in token of my good sportsmanship and my willingness to let bygones be bygones. I made it clear that the reason I had by now caught twice as many walleyes as Jim was merely due to my mastery of the technical side of Canadian lake fishing, and that luck had nothing to do with it.

Using my high school French, I graciously translated a great deal of this for the benefit of the guides. They nudged one another and roared with laughter at my remarks as they cleaned up the luncheon site. Even Jim remarked about how easy it was to blend two cultures given my gift of tongues. Everyone laughed, and with soaring spirits, we took off across the lake.

The guide had put a new line on Jim's reel. But, seeing how chagrined he was at my mastery of the sport, I insisted on spending the rest of the day pointing out the subtleties of trolling to him. And I even went so far as to enjoy part of a can of beer. By now Jim had recovered his effervescent good spirits—largely because I insisted that he tell me the secrets of his side-arm casting technique, and because I promised him I would master it on the chance we might some day fish together again.

As we readied for bed that night I found myself struggling with a major problem. Would it ever be possible for me to bend my personal credo of "the whole truth and nothing but the truth" enough so that some day I could sit down and write about fishing the way the professional writers do? My last thought that night was to promise myself that I'd get hold of, say, Ernie Schwiebert and find out how he made the moral compromise. He doesn't seem to be suffering unduly.

A CHRISTMAS LIST

I𝐅 𝐓𝐇𝐈𝐍𝐆𝐒 𝐑𝐔𝐍 true to my previous performance record, almost certainly all my Christmas shopping will be done late in the day on Christmas Eve when everything left in the stores is too big, too small and too expensive.

And, like every other year, I'll swear to myself that I'm really old enough to admit to myself that I ought to start making lists. Actually, I did start making lists this fall, when I discovered that I really couldn't pack for a trip without forgetting a lot of essentials; arriving someplace with something like eight pairs of socks and one shirt.

To be truthful, I have been putting off making lists only because my wife has been nagging me to do it. I always accused her of being one of those people who are constantly making lists in the belief that by writing a chore down it seems half done already and maybe will even completely go away. Now that I've started, in a modest way, writing *things to do* or *things to take*, I find that a lot of them end up as unnecessary.

Well, long-term practicality just isn't in me anyway but the current effort at list making has had a little fringe benefit that I didn't realize was there.

I began to find myself making up *imaginary* lists. I mean I'd find myself making up lists for trips and places I wasn't really going to take or see. I began writing down what turned out to be nothing more than daydreams . . . and taking more than a little pleasure in doing it.

I remember years ago writing imaginary orders to Sears Roebuck when I dreamed of going off to some unspecific destination called "North" and making my living trapping. I'd poke through the catalog and see myself skinning mink by lantern light and write down "two kerosene lanterns, six extra wicks."

The fact that I find myself going back to doing more or less the same sort of thing several handsful of years later doesn't say too much about my ability to ever grow up . . . but a little harmless daydreaming about some things we never got to do ought to be allowed a fellow now and then. I'm sure I got more mink and marten thumbing through a catalog by lantern light in my upstairs room than I ever would have outsmarted any other way. And I was never in much danger of freezing to death in forsaken arctic wastes as long as Mom was downstairs willing to cook up a cup of hot cocoa for a tired trapper.

I find now that I get a lot less tired and miss a lot fewer shots working over a list than I do working over some thick alder cover anyway. (That's from my list that I made when I was wishing I was getting ready to go off to New Brunswick last September.) In real life I'd be certain to forget my alarm clock—but there it is right on top of my list. And both hunting coats: the sleeveless vest and the old canvas one. I find that I have noted to bring a dog whistle for each coat. That's good. I usually really have none—or the old one that's cracked where I got mad at old Tippy and bit it. My list also covers tobacco: both smoking and chewing. In reality, I usually end up buying some off-brands of both that I don't like in some crossroads store. "Gloves"—I always end up hunting with just one—the wrong one. (If it's a real old glove for the right hand you can turn it inside out and wear it on the left.) "Socks"—I'm always good on bringing socks. "Red bandanna handkerchiefs"—I'm not so good on those and often end up with a pocket full of toilet paper to blow my runny nose. "Shooting glasses"—I'm a firm believer in always wearing glasses in the field but since I don't wear glasses every day I invariably forget them.

"Boots"—very good on boots. Two pair: the old leather ones and the leather-top rubbers. Sometimes hippers that I slop around in because everybody loses the straps that fasten the tops to your belt. "Bird gun"—very tough decision because I have two favorites, both 16-gauge. On imaginary trips I always take both. On real trips I sort of alternate. "Shells"—three boxes of light 8s. If I run out of shells—and do I!—you can bet that the local hardware store only has one box of 16s left. They were made by the Union Metallic Cartridge Company or date back to the same period, and they'll be either No. 4 or No. 5. And express loads, of course, that somebody ordered twenty years ago to shoot the fox that was getting into his white leghorns.

There are several things that I always forget—list or no list. Extra bootlaces is one, and you just know the old ones will both break the first morning out when you're already late and everybody's hollering at you to hurry up. "Suspenders"—because my wife takes them off when she launders my britches and never buttons them back on; I almost never notice they're missing until it's too late. "Dog leashes"—I always try to leave one in my hunting coat because they are as forgettable as anything. Maybe more so. And somehow I always turn up with a couple of things that I never seem to lose or forget—and that I have never had any use for: a screwdriver and a shotshell extractor that someone once brought me from England. Never pipe cleaners.

And never a sharp knife. But that's the nice thing about making lists—and the warm and pleasant difference between dreams and reality—you can always go back and start over and do it right without missing a meal, or bumming tobacco or tying a third knot in a bootlace.

As shiftless as I am, with or without lists, I have a good idea for a Christmas present for folks that aren't quite young. And that's a pup. A lot of people think that only kids should get a puppy—but a youngster is only someone else's puppy as it is. I think that puppies are fine indeed for the little guys, but when things get a little lonely for some people in their winter season, a pup is a great way to get them feeling young. A pup is a perfect blend of love and worry. A pup brings a happy sense of purpose and adventure for all the days to come. A pup can make the aches and pains of time fade away by just watching him worry a bone out from under the good chair. A pup asleep on the foot of the bed is the perfect guardian against the fears of the night. A pup is a baby that takes care of you . . . a mischievous reason for wanting to see tomorrow . . . an excuse for a walk in a soft rain . . . a reason to laugh again . . . even someone special to cook for.

Nothing can so quicken the gait toward the kitchen door than a puppy waiting inside to say "welcome."

A soft nose pressing me under the chin and a pair of deep brown eyes that really need me to make them sparkle is about as much in the way of love as a man can ordinarily handle.

I hope someday someone remembers this old dog with kindness and gives me to a puppy for Christmas.

SKILL—AND THE LACK OF IT

THE LEGENDARY voice at eventide too rarely cries, "Well done, well done," for the likes of us.

Where are the public tributes for the man who, after missing varied and sundry ruffed grouse for three seasons running, finally comes home with a day's limit? Who sings our praises when we bag ten mourning doves with only one box of shells? Where are the hymns of the multitude when our home-trained retriever perfectly marks a long fall so we don't have to stand at the edge of the water chucking empty shell cases at the carcass? Listen hard, my friend, my fellow low-achiever, for all we are ever going to hear is the sound of one hand clapping.

The only patches we wear are mute badges on our hip boots and britches that testify to the fact that we can't bend low enough any more to ease between strands of barbed wire.

SKILL—AND THE LACK OF IT

I'm sure that the great Scorekeeper in the sky has dutifully noted that Hill has fired a zillion shells trying to get 25 straight at anything, has spent enough time picking out backlashes to have earned a Ph.D. in economics at Harvard, and piddled away enough energy fooling around with skylarking bird dogs to light the city of Los Angeles for a week. If I ever do succeed in breaking 25 trap targets, getting a bird dog to at least look back when I shout or making six or eight successive casts without cataclysm, will tears come to anyone's eyes except mine? Or will the observant cynic merely murmur, "It's about time." There is no prize for guessing the right answer.

Someone ought to make up a simple certificate for the likes of us. It ought to have some bird dogs in the corner and some crossed shotguns and a couple of nice-looking decoys. At the top would be a blank space for our name and the date of the year.

Be it known to all present that —————— *is hereby recognized for his superb sportsmanship in the year* ——. *For having never forgotten his Thermos in the diner where everyone else is always leaving theirs. For being the scorekeeper in all sorts of rain and cold at his gun club during shoot-offs that he was never good enough to be in. For praising friends' dogs only slightly less biddable than his own. For pointing out rising bass to fellows who can cast better and farther. For always carrying boot patches, dry matches, extra tobacco, cards and candy bars. For never failing to say "fine shot" when someone wiped his eye on quail. For always buying his share of the gas, remembering to bring a map and being ready to go when he said he would. For always helping clean fish, pluck birds and dress game that was usually taken by others. For his ability to call someone else's wife and be believed when he said they had a flat and would be somewhat later than expected.*

The words can vary accordingly, and it ought to have a

couple of nice-looking seals on the bottom and some handwriting that looks like a signature . . . maybe even your own.

One of my many low-achieving acquaintances has built up quite a reputation (completely unearned) on the basis of framed snapshots. He's got pictures of himself standing in front of the trap club next to a guy holding out a trophy that weighs eighty pounds—and it sort of looks like he's being handed the trophy. When questioned, a rare occurrence, he merely says that the trophy is really too big, isn't it . . . implying that that's the reason it isn't sitting on the mantel.

He's got pictures of himself behind a magnificent pointer in a classic point. That one's labeled "My Pride"—fine, except it isn't his dog. He's on one end of a stringer of walleyes that are built like stovepipes . . . none of which fell to his shaky trolling. It's not a bad technique and I know that even his wife doesn't know the exact truth except for the dog, and he's gotten by that one with some story about helping train it that seems reasonable because he's got a shelfful of dog books. Another friend has a few fired shotgun shells encased in plastic. They don't stand for anything but everyone assumes that they signify 100 straight or something akin.

I really like these guys and hold no ill feeling whatsoever. They believe, really and truly, that except for some celestial phenomenon like sunspots or cosmic rays that they would surely have gone 25, or their dog might actually have held still long enough on point to have had his picture taken. Hell, I've got a couple of pictures like that myself. And only if you look very carefully at my trap jacket will you notice they're all patches that merely testify to membership and the like—never achievement.

You know people that are always saying, "What would your world be like if you were able to go out and break 250 straight?" Well, I know a couple of guys who can go out and break 250 straight, and I never saw one of them come off the line complaining of being bored with it all. I sort of agree that things would be a little sorry if we were all first-rate . . . but every once in a while I'm moved to hope that there might be room for at least one more, and I'm ready to volunteer.

I blame a lot of my shooting inadequacies (especially to my wife) on the fact that I really never had the right gun—and as luck would have it (my luck!) she was with me when I met Paul Laporte, then captain of the All-America Skeet Team. I instantly got to talking about guns and Paul handed me his. Guess what—it's exactly like mine. Same make, same grade, same stock dimensions, same choke, same everything. My wife, knowing this, only smiled.

Now a lot of people would find this a very difficult hurdle indeed, as I did at first. But as I got dwelling on it—looking for a way around—about all I could get a handle on was the old saw about one man's meat being another man's poison. Slim, I'll grant, but I was in a pretty tight corner. Suffice it to say that I presently own more than one skeet gun and more than one trap gun. Further add that this has more than once come up in family discussions. But I have a plan that involves "borrowing" a gun or so that I'm now about to try. I am, further, aware that eyebrows will rise, my probity will be under questioning and I will end up having to buy four dining-room chairs because borrowed guns don't cost anything, do they? They say that every man has his price—maybe mine's just another new shotgun. . . .

I think it was Oscar Wilde who wittily described foxhunting as "the unspeakable in pursuit of the uneatable." One might paraphrase it to fit our search for the magic as "the beaten in pursuit of the unbeatable." Well, maybe tomorrow will be a little different. The borrowed gun will chip a bird or two more than our average. Daisy will tire out early and we will get a bird or two over a point. And by pushing it a bit we could even hope to draw a third that matches one of the two low pair we're always holding

113

. . . just in case. I'm ready to trade *lucky* for *good,* at gunning, dogs or cards. It's not that I'm uncomfortable sitting down there below the salt, but I'd sure like to end up, just every so often, with the big half of the wishbone.

GEESE AND MEN

THE ONE KIND of gunning that I look forward to with the most anticipation and bank on with the most mixed emotions are the days I spend with Canada geese.

I like offshore blinds, muddy grainfield pits and being hunkered down in a ditch. I like hip boots, a necklace of calls and the heft of a three-inch magnum shell. I like warm down parkas and the taste of bad weather. I like the kind of wind I can lean into and the slap of sleet on my earflaps. I like the promise of dawn and the memories that come with sunset. I like oversized decoys, boats I can pole and the excitement in the thumping of a Labrador's tail. I like the smell of salt water, gunpowder and wet dogs. I like the wonder and the waiting. I'm a goose hunter.

What other creature is always prefixed with the word "wild"? What other creature combines such mysteries of sight and sound? A flock of geese seems to be in command of the sky and their arrogant trumpeting calls our attention to the passage of majesty.

A friend of mine said that the passing of geese always filled him with wonder because they seem to come from a place that only they really know about. A place that could only exist in his imagination—a place that was on no earthly map—a place as gray and mysterious as the geese themselves. A place no human eye was fit to see.

When folks say "as silly as a goose" I'm sure they don't refer to the Canada. The geese I hang around with have been outsmarting me for years. They either fly ten yards out of range over the center of my blind all day—honking constantly to make sure I know they're there—or pass just over my head so silently that I never know they've been too close until they're too far away.

Geese not only outsmart me, they scare me. I can go through more shells with less effect in a goose blind than anyone else I know. But I'm learning. One thing I've learned is that the goose I discover sitting, swimming around in the decoys, is as safe as a goose sailing along in the stratosphere. I remember a blue-finger morning that was chunking sleet the size of pea coal when I discovered that somehow a goose had slipped in among the blocks about thirty yards from the blind. I nudged the old buddy next to me, pointed out the bird and whispered the plan: He should stand up, flush the goose, then take him. He rose up according to plan and the goose flushed according to plan. Carefully taking his time, carefully swinging through, he emptied three loads of magnum 2s six feet, ten feet and fifteen feet behind the bird. That's pretty good shooting under the circumstances. I almost never get much closer than twenty feet. But, as I said, I'm getting smarter. I would never take a chance on that shot—too easy—to miss a fine goose.

116

GEESE AND MEN

A perfect goose day is not only a test of skill, but more importantly an exhibition of enthusiasm and pure endurance. At its best the day must be marginal for human life. When I'm shivering under my down pants, down shirt, down vest, down coat and my feet are cold enough to frost a twenty-gallon martini then I know I'm doing the right thing, in the right place at the right time. Just add the frosting of a thirty-knot snowstorm and remind me that I've left my Thermos of tea and my handwarmer four miles away back in the car.

I admit that a good goose hunter has to be smarter than the goose. I will also admit that I'm not. I only get the dumb ones on my dining-room table, with lots of plum jelly on the side. That leaves the smarter ones for the other guys, which is as it should be since most of the other guys I know can call better, shoot better and know more than one way of putting out decoys. They don't leave their hot tea in the diner and they can make a handwarmer stay lit. Their lighters always work and their tobacco never gets soaked.

I don't know too much about a lot of things, but most of all I don't understand geese. I can't tell a goose from a gander unless I see one laying eggs. I don't know why I can miss a nine-pound bird flying about ten miles an hour in a headwind when I can bring down a pair of teal hitting the speed of sound in the other direction. I don't understand why I can build a blind so perfectly hidden that even I have trouble finding it and flock after flock will flare away to circle low over the hide across the cove where there are two guys sitting out front drinking coffee.

I don't know why I'd rather sit—semi-submerged in a flooded pit blind that I've walked two hours through mud to get to, carrying enough stores for a trans-Arctic trek—and never fire a shot and talk all night about the wonderful day I had after geese, than take my limit of a lot of other stuff. It's just because I'm a goose hunter. But if you're a goose hunter too, you'll understand.

117

It's not the hunting—it's the geese, and if that's where they are, that's where we'll be. And we'll be listening to try to come to understand what it is that the geese are so mournfully tolling. I believe that being there is important. And every so often—too seldom, too seldom—I believe I can hear the story in the chanting of a single goose. I think he's talking about the same things old men like us will like to talk about—to anyone or anything that will listen.

They talk about old friends, strange lands and storms . . . how no one pays them any mind . . . about the distances that he must travel to return where he belongs.

And then I think about my friends and storms and the distances that I have yet to go—and for a little while there in the weather and the biting wind, I know that there is more in common, goose and man, man and man, than we care to think.

HOW MANY GUNS ARE ENOUGH?

Dear Ms. Johnson:

Thank you very much for your most pleasant letter. I always enjoy hearing from ladies, and of course, I'm delighted to try to answer your question—as I believe I can see the situation that lies behind it.

You ask me, "How many guns do you have?" And I suspect that you feel the man in your life is reaching a level that you, in your innocence, feel is sufficient, or perhaps overabundant.

Let me answer your question first from a more realistic angle, the angle that I, like most men, regretfully have to face every day of my life. What are the guns that I *don't* have!

I do not own, nor have I had the opportunity to own—which goes without saying—a good side-by-side .470 double rifle. I often bring this up at home when my own wife remarks that I seem a bit peckish or morose. Her predictable response is that I don't have any earthly use for a .470 double, a .500 double or a .577 double. She doesn't have any use for a profile like Raquel Welch either, but that doesn't mean she wouldn't like it. Suppose someone asked me to go to Africa . . . what would I say? Suppose, worse yet, that a guest asked to see my double rifle, assuming that any right-thinking sportsman would own one, and I have to stand there shifting uneasily from one foot to another making up very transparent excuses like, "It's back in London having the sears hardened." I can only compare it to a man going through life without a good blue suit; it's that basic.

Worse yet, I'm probably the only person in the group I regularly associate with that doesn't own a .30-06. Most of my friends own several, luckily, and they would never think of asking about mine any more than they would insist on seeing my marriage license. (I assume your husband has both.)

I do not even own a .243, a .22 Hornet (near the top of my must list!), a .300 H&H or even the common 7mm magnum. I don't mean to sound like Oliver Twist pleading for more porridge, nor do I mean to imply that since your man has, very likely, all of these and more, that he is among the blessed. I am merely stating the unpleasant facts—there are people like that, you know, and I fear I am one of "those."

I could go on, but rather than reduce you to a state of uncontrolled pity where you start sneaking me duplicates from your husband's basic collection, let me shift you away from the sordid confession that I have no wherewithal to collect rhino, nothing for 300-yard antelope, no match target piece, and I am drawing zero in the area that my friend Tony Dyer from Nairobi would classify as a decent "medium rifle."

Far worse is my assembly (a stroke of humor here in that word) of basic shotguns. Let us begin by saying that if I were invited tomorrow to partake in a round of skeet involving the .410

or the 28-gauge I would have to plead a sick headache or say that I had just finished washing my hair.

Even as the 12th of August comes near, I must refuse to open my mail or answer the phone. The 12th, as you know, is the traditional opening day of grouse shooting in Scotland, and as you might have already guessed, I have nothing that remotely resembles the matched pair of 12-bores that are as mandatory for a gentleman gun as a heather-shade pair of shooting knickers.

I could too easily go on, but I'm sure you have your problems and don't need a recitation of mine. You might fairly say that I'm dodging your question, which in a way I am, but there is a second, and more realistic answer.

A close reading of much of shooting's modern literature reveals the fact that only two men in the world have enough guns. One is a Middle East oil potentate who patterns his Purdeys on the rear door of a special Rolls-Royce made especially for this function. (It's a fine way to get a two-dimensional look at a shot pattern, as you can closely simulate the speed of flight of most game birds and check the effect of density as well as the length of effective shot-stringing.)

The other is a bearded writer for an outdoor publication, who will be instantly identified by merely mentioning he is a worse shot than I am.

Guns, like love, cannot be measured with numbers. It's common knowledge to the student of modern sociology that the more guns a man owns the more happily married he tends to be.

I believe that the divorce rate of men who own more than one double rifle, or sidelock shotgun, in a high grade of course, is virtually nil. This is because today's extremely intelligent and sensitive liberated woman has discovered that a highly engraved Holland or Churchill, as a love token, has proven to quickly dry the tears of the most deeply hurt husband.

In my own case, when I embraced the common twins, youth

121

and poverty, my wife set out our meager holiday dinners around a table whose centerpiece was a cleverly arranged motif of red and green 2¾ No. 8 trap loads, knowing that such a little gift would be far more cheering to my humble spirit than the more perishable and overly feminine flowers or fruit.

I'm sure that if you read between the lines, you'll find that the common term "shotgun wedding" has its real origin in a far different context than used today. Let's hope that the original meaning returns to warm our customs.

I, for one, still believe in the traditional dowry. And, since I have a brace of daughters, I pass up no opportunity to pick up another gun to enhance their chances of "good marriages" when the time comes. They seem perfectly willing to forego the shallow and passing need for new shoes and warm clothes knowing that their father is thinking ahead for their more important welfare in the future. And I know that there are a lot of fathers out there just like me. There'll be at least a dozen at any trap club, come any Sunday, making sure that their future sons-in-law will get shotguns that they know will please them, because they've used it and used it often.

I hope, in my circuitous way, I have been of some help to you. Let me remind you that the average outdoorsman is a very sensitive man. He does not want to embarrass his wife and family by going off on an elk hunt, let's say, unless he has a good .270, a .7mm Magnum or a decent .375. Nor should we be misled by the fact that he shoots trap with a 4-grade Ithaca single-barrel—what happens at the gun club when the fellows try to cajole him into a round of doubles? Does he beg off, saying that he forgot to bring the cashmere jacket his wife bought him for doubles, or does he snap open the brass locks of a top-grain leather trunk case and bring forth a high-grade over-and-under with "To G.A.H. from M.E.H." engraved on the receiver? Is he a well-appreciated husband or just another beast of burden? I leave that to you, my gentle reader.

May you happily look forward to the day when you can paraphrase the famous couplet of Elizabeth Barrett Browning: "How do I love thee? Let me count the guns . . ."

GREAT MORNING

I GUESS I'VE BEEN deer hunting for something over thirty years, and I suppose I've killed my fair share of deer. I can look back on many moments when everything seemed to come alive at the fleeting footfall of a buck—his very awareness made the forest ring with silence. These times are everlasting in the memory— but even more memorable are the times when I've been really warm.

Deer hunting and subzero weather seem to go hand in hand in my part of the East. And I doubt it has ever been colder on an opening day than the year I got my very first buck.

I woke up that morning about four and crept downstairs to start the fire in the kitchen stove. About the time the fire got going good, the men began to drift in from early-morning chores. The kitchen smelled wonderful once all the men had gotten warm. The air was heavy with woodsmoke, tobacco, odors of dog and barnyard. And the not-so-secret source of most of these damp smells was the long-lost and wonderfully warm felt boots. Felt boots were a standard item in every farmer's wardrobe. If you remember, they were made in two parts. A long, thick, felt, socklike affair that came to the knee was covered by a separate heavy rubber shoe that came just above the ankle and fastened by two or three metal buckles. They were heavy as hell—but they were warm! Naturally I had a pair. I also had on a heavy woolen union suit (over a pair of regular underwear), two pair of heavy bib overalls, I forget how many shirts, and topping all this was a blanket-lined denim coat we called an "overall jacket."

My grandfather put me on the first stand, behind a giant fallen chestnut log. I was told to stay put.

"What if I shoot a deer?" I asked, positive that I would.

"Stay put," was the answer.

And stay put I did. I really didn't have too much choice. Wrapped all around me was a giant horse blanket, the kind with a raft of buckles and straps on it. Nestled between my legs was a kerosene hand lantern. I sat there like a human tent with my own personal furnace going. In those days we didn't worry too much about a deer smelling any of us. I guess because we all smelled like so many horses and cows ourselves. If I didn't smell like a horse, it wasn't the fault of the blanket and the kerosene lamp forcing the odor out for a couple of country miles. I probably would have smelled like a horse anyway—and the outfit was plenty of insurance. The real point of all this is the absolute fact that I was deliciously warm. I was more than warm—I was downright cozy. By the time the sun had risen completely over the horizon I had, of course, eaten all my lunch.

Grandpa came by about ten o'clock and asked me how I was. I was just fine and told him so, adding that I was getting a little hungry. He gave me a couple of sandwiches and a handful of cookies that must have weighed a quarter of a pound apiece, and told me again to stay put. I don't think I could have gotten out of that rig if I'd wanted to, but I promised him, and off he went again.

Under the blanket I held my most cherished possession—an old 1897 Winchester pump gun. It wasn't really mine. Pop had borrowed it for me to use. The thirty-inch full-choke barrel stuck up out of the blanket like a chimney, and I kept swiveling it around as best I could without disturbing the oven arrangement. I can tell you, I was mighty eager to use it.

Along about noon I was about half asleep from so much food and the warmth from the old lantern when a sharp crack of a broken twig brought my eyes open. Against the snow, about a quarter-mile off through the woods, I could see the four legs of a deer cautiously working its way down toward my stand. Buck or doe, I couldn't be sure because of the hazel and birch thickets between us. As slowly as I could I eased the old '97 up out of the blanket and across the chestnut log and began following the legs of that deer closer toward me through the woods.

About fifty yards directly in front of me was a tiny brook with a clearing or two on the other side, along the bank. With absolute certainty, the deer—whatever it was—was heading down toward one of those clearings. I eased the hammer back on the Winchester with a very shaky thumb; buck fever was coming on a little faster than the deer. But if I had seen this sight once in my dreams and my imagination, I'd seen it a thousand times.

I couldn't take my eyes off those four legs . . . three or four more steps, and he'd be in the clearing by the brook. And suddenly there he was! A buck—a big curving Y. Somehow as the barrel swung back and forth over the clearing I managed to shoot. Just one shot. I don't believe I could have pumped that gun if my life depended on it. At the shot the buck twitched, stepped carefully back from the brook and just as cautiously as he had

126

come down began to walk away as I helplessly watched him. I really never thought of the second shell (I was only allowed to have two buckshot). With a feeling of abject shame, I saw him disappear into the woods. I had missed him. How would I ever tell Grandpa and Pop?

Well, I sat there feeling lower than a cricket's knee. If I hadn't been eleven, I might have cried. Sooner or later, I knew, the hard part had to come—in the form of my father, and it wasn't fifteen minutes until he showed up. He was kind of smiling, as I remember it.

"You shoot?" he asked.

I nodded.

"Where's the dead deer?"

I said there wasn't any dead deer; that he had just walked away.

"Which way did he walk?"

"Around behind that big beech tree was the last I saw," I told him, fearful that I'd be dealt with pretty harshly for wasting a shell.

"Well, you'd better come along and show me," Pop said, and uncovered me, blew out the lantern and started off toward the beech tree. He made me unload the gun, and I felt pretty small as I shucked out the empty shell that had sat in the chamber, forgotten. I put the other shell in my pocket and trudged along behind him.

I should have suspected something when he quickened his pace as we passed the spot where I had last seen the buck, but deep in misery and head down I just tried to walk in his tracks and keep up. I almost fell over the deer.

"This is him, isn't it?" he said, standing by a fallen fork horn, about fifty yards beyond the big beech.

"Yep," I said, trying to indicate by my tone of voice that I wasn't the most surprised person in the world.

127

"Well, boy, you'd better drag him down by the brook so's we can clean him out."

I guess I could have dragged a bull moose right then, and drag I did, right into the flowing water where we cleaned and washed him out.

By the time the other men had gathered, and I told how I had shot my first deer, the carcass had frozen solid. Grandpa had come along and gathered up my blanket and lantern and asked me if I'd been warm enough. I said I had, but that I was getting mighty cold again.

"Here, boy," he said, handing me a two-foot loop of rope, "warmest thing in the world."

"How's that going to keep me warm?" I asked.

"Simple," he said, "just wrap one end around the deer's neck and the other around your hand and start walking toward the wagon."

Well, I miss the old felt boots, and I still think the blanket—provided it smells like a dapple-gray—and the lantern are pretty comforting. But to really keep a deer hunter warm, there's nothing like a two-foot rope around a man's hand, with a sleek December buck on the other end.

THE COMPLEAT ANGLER: ALMOST

NEXT TIME you're fishing and need pliers or leader clippers and you don't have them—blame my dentist.

I will admit that dentists have done more for me than I have for them—on the whole. I will further admit that I never met a dentist I didn't like; they serve only the finest whiskey, the most delicate caviar, and their wines are legendary. And rather than treat dentists as curiosities only to be seen on special occasions like symphonies or museums, I have actually made friends with several and treat them as I would any ordinary human being.

But the remark that James Thurber once made about piano players—that they have no imagination—goes double for dentists, or at least mine.

It all started last spring when a close friend, whose ordinary words about me are as pleasurable to the ear as honey is to the tongue, remarked that my fly-rod technique reminded him of a blind man trying to kill a mouse with a broom handle. Since I am a most honest fellow, well aware that I am "closer to the French than to the angels" as Mark Twain would say, I was not offended, but immediately called up Leigh Perkins, who runs things at the Orvis Company, and told him it was an emergency situation and could they take another patient in the fly-fishing school immediately. Having caught Leigh by surprise, he sort of said "yes" and off I went for a most enjoyable and informative few days.

Like most people who visit the Orvis store you find loads of gear that you suddenly discover you can no longer live without. Fly threaders, hook hones, leader straighteners and various odds and ends that you stuff in your fly-jacket pockets or hang on little reels from your vest. It was during one of these purchases that I felt a twinge in a rear molar and a flash of nearly divine inspiration flooded my being. I made a hurried excuse and used one of the office phones to call my dentist and make an appointment for the same afternoon I planned on arriving home.

It so happens that my dentist friend is also an avid fly-fisherman. And, like all avid fly-fishermen, a man who has seen the improbable and the unusual often and has become impervious to being shocked or startled.

I settled myself down in his chair and told him of my adventures at the Orvis school. I went on to describe the various gadgets that fly-fishermen adorn themselves with and he nodded in agreement, having bought all of them himself at one time or another.

Then I told him of how in the very act of buying my fifteenth or twentieth leader clipper I had this incredibly brilliant idea: Instead of merely plugging my nagging molar with whatever dentists plug molars with, I wanted it and the tooth above fitted out with hard grooved caps so they could function like pliers for clamping split-shot and the like. Further, I said, I wanted my top and bottom front teeth fitted out with sharp edges so I could bite through 20-pound mono, or even a WF-9F line.

A coating of Carborundum on an incisor and I would have a hook hone with me at all times—and who *ever* has a hook hone when he wants one? Bill took to the idea right off and even began suggesting that I could go on and have leader-straightening pads on the other molars, and tippet gauges fitted in the crevices between my lower teeth. He began making little drawings and lists of material he'd need when a touch of remorse crossed his face. He couldn't go through with it, he said, because of all the people who made a living making all the stuff fly-fishermen like to buy to hang on their clothes. And after a little thought, I had to agree. Buying things is one of the major reasons anyone in his right mind takes up fly-fishing in the first place. No one needs all that stuff just to catch trout; it gets in the way, gets lost, and there are literally dozens of ways to take trout that are far easier and more effective than artificial flies. Tackle companies would suffer such a loss of business that they wouldn't be able to send out their catalogs. What would fishermen read if it weren't for the catalogs? What would they do with their money? How would they spend their vacations if they couldn't travel around and see what other fishermen had pinned to their hats and vests?

Bill brightened a bit when I suggested that maybe tackle companies would take on a group of dentists and outfit fishermen the way I suggested. Then fishermen could ask each other, "Who's your dentist? Orvis? Dan Bailey? Hardy? Fenwick? Garcia?"

But finally Bill demurred. "All their wives would object to the husbands' running around with all that hardware in their mouths. Their kids would think they looked funny."

"Wives all object to their husbands fishing all the time anyway, and all their kids think the old man is around the bend as it is. What difference does it make?" I asked him.

"Look," he said, "most fly-fishermen are also bird hunters, aren't they?"

"All the ones I know are," I agreed.

"Well, the next thing that would happen is that they'd want a set of interchangeable tools. One guy would want his wisdoms made into a dog whistle because he never remembers to carry one. Another would insist he be fitted with a bottle opener, somebody else would want his false tooth shaped like a screwdriver—there's no telling where it would end. People might even start making odd remarks about dentists in general, and the whole profession would be down on me. Let's just put it down as one of your crazy ideas and forget the whole thing."

"Okay," I said, "but don't forget that it intrigued you for a while too."

Bill nodded and began cementing up the molar hole that had gotten the idea born in the first place. When he finished, he began using some dental floss to clean up the area, and when I mentioned that the floss was about 1X and that maybe some smart dental-supply company could do something about that he shooed me out of his office.

Well, they say no man is a prophet in his own country, but I wish I could foresee the day that nature looks more kindly on the fisherman, since he is ill adapted to his tasks. He cannot function without a battery of tools and aids. Compared to the osprey or the otter, as a fish-getter he is a joke.

Yet, stout fellow that he is, he perseveres. Nature has not given him eyes to tie on No. 20 flies, nor has she given him the dexterity to tie knots, the agility to wade fast water or the brains to outwit a trout he has just seen feeding on the filter of a tossed-away cigarette.

His fellowman has only, so far, given him the basics of chest waders, whiskey, tobacco and bug spray. Not a bad start, but we leave him clanking and rattling behind a vast arsenal of shears, pliers and other rusting impedimenta—basically a trusting, patient being hoping against all odds to return home with something to justify his avoidance of paternal responsibilities and yard work.

For a fleeting moment in time, I felt that my dental canyons had served the same purpose that the apple did for Sir Isaac Newton: further equipping man to enjoy his place in a too often bewildering environment.

It is apparently not to be. The dreams of fame fade away, and the hope of service to my fellow sportsmen still lies where it first began—in my constant demonstrations of lack of proficiency designed to make nearly anyone who can chew gum and walk at the same time look like an Olympian by comparison.

A MILLION DOLLARS

THERE'S A RATHER well-known short story about two office girls who played a game at lunch called "What would you do if you had a million dollars?" One day they started their game just as they were passing the window of a famous New York jewelry store, and one of them noticed a magnificent diamond necklace in the window. "I'd start off buying that," she said. But they began to argue about how much such a necklace could be until they finally went in and asked. The salesman smiled at such an unlikely pair shopping for diamonds but graciously showed them the price tag: $1,200,000.

I'll admit that thinking about what I'd do if I were "rich" takes up more of my time than it should; time that should be spent replacing shingles on my leaking roof or digging a drainage ditch in my flooded field . . . chores that I'm well aware do not eat up too much time of those more well-to-do.

But do you realize how much the cost of being rich has gone up? It's getting so bad that a reasonable man today can hardly afford to daydream without getting embarrassed.

I felt pretty comfortable dreaming about owning a side-by-side Purdey or Holland when they only cost $2,500, but now that the base price has moved up to about $5,000 with a three- to four-year wait, I simply can't afford it.

A friend just sold a beautiful Leonard fly rod for $500, and all the while I'd been dreaming of owning one at the imaginary price of about $150. I suddenly felt like Rip Van Winkle!

You've been dreaming of fishing for Atlantic salmon in Norway for about $1,500 a week? Try doubling that, you're still dreaming at the old prices. How about a safari in Africa with a first-class hunter for $200 a day? You might as well ask the orchestra to play you a lindy hop or try to find a nice comfortable pair of high-button dress shoes to wear.

The pipes I used to like, and saved for, because they were good buys even at the incredible price of $12 now start at around $50. My old nickel paper of tobacco costs 35¢.

About the only thing we can keep down to a reasonable level is our income—that doesn't seem to have gotten involved with inflation.

So I've had to lay back a bit on dreaming and put more effort into handling the day-to-day. I always made a small thing about being fairly well dressed for bird hunting. That is, being neat and clean, not wearing overalls and galoshes. But my favorite hunting pants that I used to go through at the rate of two pair a season, at about $15 a pair, now start at twice that. Which means I've got to pay a lot more attention to the width of the strands in barbed-wire fences and be a bit more strict with my dogs on retrieving in briars.

I'm perfectly willing, as usual, to let my thoughts wander to what might have been, but considerably scaled down; reality is about as far as the mind can travel today without being overly taxed—in more ways than one.

Money being out of the question—the opportunity's now denied us, we come to the hoarding of time, and find, sadly, that time as well has sifted through our fingers like the sands of a broken hourglass. Yet to dream a bit about it is possible, but as with money, still tinged by sadness.

We have all looked ahead to owning time that could be spent in lieu of other commodities. Time to boil a few pine knots to mold into decoy heads. Time to fine-hone a pointing dog. Time to checker a stock, work a knife from a file and ax out a paddle. Time to learn to tie flies. Time to craft a rod or make a boat. And time to learn to use them well. Time to see where the river sprang from a spring, time to see past the horizon, time to listen to the birds and smell the pines, time to see where the bear went over the mountain and see what he could see.

Remember when time was cheap? The songs we sang about it told us that we had time on our hands, that time stood still, that tomorrow would be time enough. And now we find it was not so.

Suddenly times to come have become times past, and we must hoard it and spend it as cautiously as the tag ends of a small inheritance . . . which is what it really was all along—except no one told us.

So we find now that the skills we dreamed of are scant and awkward. The time came to choose between spending money or time, and most of us chose money—because as little as we had of it, we had more of it than time.

Our decoys, one or two or so, are pathetic, awkward birds that never came alive from wood. A dog or so was worked just enough to be called "passable" by closer friends, but the knives I use are not shaped by my hand, and my paddles have none of the warm idiosyncrasies of my carving.

I bum flies and borrow the rods I dreamed of making. The

mountain that I waited so long to cross is woven with tar roads, and the bear is a remnant from stories of others and trips to the zoo with children.

But regret cannot be bundled up like a foundling and left late at night on another's doorstep, to be someone else's responsibility. And although I did few of the things I once dreamed of—I've done a good many things that please me much.

Having made my bed, so to speak, I find myself lying in it with less discomfort than I might. Should I someday, like an ancient king, command that all my goodies be brought before me that I might survey from my counterpane what I made of my life's pleasures the panorama would not be too displeasing.

Instead of my own masterful decoys I have a handful of the real masters: Ira Jester, Captain Joseph Lincoln and Ira Hudson. A couple of knives by the likes of Loveless and Russell. A shotgun or two and a fly rod or so that I'm not ashamed to be seen with in public. I could extend the list a bit, but fearful of family reprisals and trades by my more astute friends, I forebear.

A friend of mine who was an avid and far above average golfer once overheard his boss telling someone, "You show me a man who plays to a four handicap, and I'll show you a man who doesn't give too much thought to his job."

You show me a man who has a house, badly in need of paint, a closetful of shotguns and rifles, walls covered with prints of bird dogs and sporting scenes but no furniture and an untrimmed lawn filled with retrievers, and I'll show you a man who spent his life dreaming . . . with very few regrets.

The money I've earned I've spent like a sailor on leave, and the time I promised to put in on useful endeavors I've spent skylarking with similar-minded friends; exchanging daydream for daydream about what magnificent things we would have if we were rich—and the wonderful things we would accomplish if only we ever had the time.

SANDWICHES

THEY SAY the sandwich is the result of the Earl of Sandwich using a couple of chunks of bread for a better grip on a slab of beef.

No matter, really, except I thank whoever it was—Earl or no. I'm sure I went from my bottle of formula right to some kind of sandwich, and the love affair has lasted very well.

Unhappily for the young, or so it once was, when kids grew up under the old rules, you got handed whatever sandwich someone else made. No vote, no opinion, no preference. You ate the sandwiches that your mother liked or liked to make, or what she thought was good for you, which was the worst kind of all. So, like most kids, I grew up with a variety that was basically peanut butter and homemade grape jelly alternated with cheese—except for certain Mondays which featured leftover chicken, the special occasion, fancy Sunday dinner. A rare treat occasionally came along in the form of bologna, or liverwurst. Both, I might add, real stuff, not the pallid, tasteless imitation we find lurking guiltily between layers of supermarket plastic—which you can eat by mistake and never be aware of more than a change in chewiness.

So much for my mother's basic lunchbox cuisine. My father's sandwiches, made for days out fishing or hunting, were basically onion. Onion and cheese, onion and meat or just plain onion. They were terrible to face for two reasons. One is a fact that went unheeded by him—and still does—that onions give me agonizing indigestion. Indigestion was not in my father's lexicon of recognizable or admitted childhood ailments so I just suffered or starved. The second reason, and I like the ordinary mild onion even if it does make me sick, is that somehow he, who grew our own onions, happened on a strain so virulent and caustic that it would have brought tears to the eyes of a cigar-store Indian. While I would clasp my throat and weakly cry out for water over the thin slice in my sandwich, he would frequently munch on one like an apple and deplore the weak strain that somehow managed to manifest itself in his son. Onions were good for you, and that was that. And if *any* onion was good for you, I was admonished to conjure on how good for me this one was if it brought sweat to the forehead, redness to the tips of my ears, loss of speech, double vision and something near to locomotor ataxia.

The wise man, reading this far, says the kid is a dummy. Why doesn't he make his own sandwich? And that is exactly what the kid did except for those too frequent mornings when the kid lay in bed until four-thirty and was roused and told that everything was in the car, sandwiches and all, and his father stood over him and hustled him out of the house still carrying half his clothes in his arms. (Even writing about those incendiary snacks makes me get up and knock back a Rolaid—thirty years, alas, too late to help.)

No matter how far down on the culinary scale you mark a spot for an onion-and-cheese sandwich, and I rated it only over sandwiches made of headcheese or turnips, I was often reminded, when I complained, that I was lucky we weren't poor and could afford cheese—and there were plenty I knew in the category that couldn't.

So, belching goodbye to Pop's cooking, we move up the scale several years later to the day I realized what grandmothers are for—they are there because their sons and daughters do not know how to raise children. Grandmothers know how and are very anxious to prove it. So the night, or better, a couple of days before a fishing outing in order to give her time to prepare, I would shanks' mare it over to grandma's and ask her for a lunch bag for Saturday. Grandma would set immediately to work. Grandmothers, as I hope you well remember, believed that all their grandchildren were deprived—and none of the grandchildren in my peer groups did anything to alter the opinion by so much as one homemade, quarter-pound vanilla cookie.

Friday night I would stumble home with a bag weighing about eight pounds that smelled of heaven and grandmother—both being equal in my mind yet.

The next day my father would watch with disgust as I worked through homemade creampuffs, inch-thick slices of homemade bread that held inch-thick slices of cold roast beef or pork or turkey smothered in the appropriate horseradish, applesauce or cranberry relish. There would be giant cookies, fruit, and often a slab of divinity or chocolate fudge, always deviled eggs and frequently a chicken breast or drumstick—just in case.

I am solidly in the school that believes just because you're out of doors you don't have to eat what a beaver eats. I may forget shells, those I can borrow, but I don't forget lunch. And I don't like to hunt with people who forget theirs. Instead I seek the company of civilized folk like the sainted Robert O'Byrne, who prepared the lunch for a roadside stop on a trip to Merrymeeting Bay for ducks.

His only companions were myself and my Labrador, Tippy. Finding a pleasant roadside place, we pulled in, and while I walked the dog, Bob set out our modest repast. A touch of imported sardines served as a simple *hors d'oeuvres,* leading up to cold fried chicken, thin rolled slices of beef stuffed with asparagus, cheesecake for a modest sweet, washed down by an ice-cold bottle of a crackling white wine and finished with steaming coffee on which he delicately floated a spoonful of Armagnac. Tippy's lunch was a brace of cold hamburgers and a cookie that she delicately nibbled from my fingers. And that is as close as I've ever known O'Byrne to come to a luncheon sandwich.

Wives, generally, don't make great sandwiches. Oddly enough, my vast research on the subject reveals that a woman who will eagerly turn out a chicken galantine or a Toulouse cassoulet at the slightest hint will make a sandwich out of wet lettuce and mayonnaise that has turned. Women have no basic interest in sandwiches; they are not in a homemaker's category of "good food," or maybe they are too cumbersome to be handled with delicacy. Anyway, a super selection of viands, spices and garnishes placed between a carefully selected choice of bread is man's work. So be it.

A wise and philosophical friend of mine believes that one of the moving reasons men hunt and fish and get up at weird and uncomfortable hours is so they can make the kind of sandwiches they really like for lunch: Limburger and liverwurst with tart pickle relish between hearty slices of sour rye. Cold baked beans, a thick slice of baked Virginia ham covered with sweet mustard and held together with a coarse white bread. Sliced steak, horseradish, tomato, in a poppyseed roll. Plain but filling fare. The sandwiches must be whole, not sliced, and should weigh no more or less than half a box of high-velocity duck loads.

I agree that this is a perfectly valid reason around which to center a day of sport. But what happens when we are off in a hired duck camp? The cook is the owner's wife, and we are back basically where we started with our mothers in grammar school: peanut butter and jelly and cheese, some kind of artificial cake and a stalk of celery that is as limp as a fly line or strung with nylon. Once, by a mistake nobody could explain, I got cold canvasback breast, liberally peppered and dashed with homemade mayonnaise; just once. Maybe I got the guide's sandwich by mistake. Ever notice how guides *always* find something to do somewhere else at noon? Looking to see how Charlie's guys have done, go back to town for smokes, or whatever, but they're not around as you tease your upper plate with cheap peanut butter and a wizened apple. Ever see a skinny guide? Never. That's because they're the ones in the kitchen first, taking care of Number One, while the drowsy, overworked cook slaps together six so-called sandwiches in fifty-eight seconds.

Basically, you're stuck. You're up before the stores open and home after they're closed—if there are any stores. Try sneaking a piece of your breakfast ham in a biscuit or rolled up in a cold pancake, and you get a look usually reserved for a child-molester. At duck camps there are two kinds of lunches: good ones and ones for the guests. I'm sure exceptions exist, but mostly in history or vivid imaginations.

If the Earl of Sandwich had been a duck hunter and his inspiration had hit him in the ordinary rented blind, just think of the loss to civilization; it would be as tragic as if Isaac Newton had chosen to sit and think in a field of milkweed or dandelions instead of under an apple tree. Maybe worse.

On the other hand it would be just my luck to once more get the guide's lunch, by mistake of course, and while he's away seeing what Charlie's sports have gunned, I open his battered pail and find . . . onions, and onions and cheese.

A NEW YEAR'S SONG

I'M SURE THAT even the cavemen shuddered a bit at the midwinter calling of the Great Horned Owl, for this, more than any other call, save that of the lonesome loons and wolves, has reminded all of us of the strange, dark shadows we would very gladly ignore.

But there's another way to listen to the five notes of the Great Horned Owl on a solemn and dreary February night. Think of them as a melody, signaling for the beginning of another year.

You can hear the odd musing, challenges or whatever it is that the owl has on his mind to call out into the night, almost anytime of the year, but it is in the depth of winter, when an owl seeks a mate, that the music is at its wildest peak.

I hear these awesome mutterings now with a blend of welcome for me, and a sense of regret for the unseen, small trundling things that the owls, this night, will sweep up into the crevices of their midnight-shaded trees.

Hearing these varied and unearthly sounds makes it easy to believe any of the many legends that surround the Great Horned Owl.

I know people today who believe that when an owl sits on a barn, something on the farm will shortly die. Some Indians believed (and some may yet) that the owl calls at night because it wants the soul of a person. If someone happened to be thought on the verge of death, he or she was given owl feathers to hold to keep the bird at bay.

I know it's only superstition, but when the moonlight now casts eerie shadows from my trees and the owls call, I feel a little colder and pause to linger on the number of my days.

I don't know that the owl is, in truth, any wiser than any other old bird; however, I won't argue that he seems to represent something that I don't understand—a feeling that he is telling me about another place that I have never seen.

But I must admit that I wait with longing for the coming of the new year and the calling of the owls. I—maybe because I'm a good deal of a Scot—have a stirring of some old blood with this kind of wild music—the way I get with a too-seldom glass of a heavy malt whisky and the company of bagpipers. Maybe that's what the owl call is to the rest of the animal world—the sound of warrior trumpets, the wail of pipers, the roll of martial drums. The announcement of a coming attack . . . the intimidating alarm of the strong to the small . . . a chill sound that turns the blood to ice.

A naturalist I know says he knows about twenty words of goose; that he can often tell just what the honkers are chatting about, and I believe him. But the voice of the Canada goose rolls from a bird I often watch and study. Not so the Great Horned

Owl. His voice tumbles out to singe my ear from deep inside the dark. He's not gathering his flock and giving directions for someone to do this or that. No, I believe that my Great Horned Owls are talking nighttime talk to things other than owls. I do not believe the owl tells jokes the way some birds are wont to do. He does not sing to me of love for life the way some birds are wont to do. No "Joy to the World" intent booms out from way back across the brook to lift my heart against the scudding clouds. I think he tells whoever listens—and many, many must—about doomsday and the like. He sings of terror to those who have to sit and listen—those other birds and mice and rabbits all hope, I'm sure, that the owl they hear is singing the last song that some thing will ever hear, to someone else. And then they crouch and wait and listen for the sudden silence punctuated by a shriek.

I have no doubt that now and then, when I hear my midwinter ghosts, they sing of love and such to other owls, but the passion of the Great Horned Owl is somehow foreign to my concept of affection. Beneath the owls' love nest in a sycamore close by is a ring of skulls and bones—love offerings from the hunter to his brooding mate—not needfully more grisly than two robins tugging at a worm or a wren picking at an ant, but nonetheless it always strikes a different mood in me, because I know that those Great Horned birds will stoop my pup or cat, and should I let my soft-eyed hens stay out at night, I'll find their feathers drifting on the lawn come morning.

Yet among themselves these great big creatures have close bonds and loyal feelings too. Some years ago, a Great Horned Owl was hurt and sitting on the lawn beneath her tree. With an incredible clumsiness she managed to climb the trunk and work her way out to the middle of the longest limb. And there she sat for several days while her mate hovered close to protect her from my barking dogs. He would bring her tidbits of mice from daytime hunts, and drop them in her clacking beak, and but for these brief flights he never left her side. Then one morning they were both gone and neither seen again by day.

The word "owl" comes from an old Anglo-Saxon word that describes the hooting sound—the same root as our word "howl." The owl cannot rotate his eyes so he swivels his head almost completely around. Although he hunts at night, he can see just as well by day. My friend Angus Cameron in his marvelous book on owls, *The Nightwatchers,* says that the Great Horned Owl is very fond of killing and eating skunks, and many of them carry the characteristic odor.

I've never seen an owl working on a skunk sandwich—but you'll never catch me working over roast owl and gravy in any event. I know people who have eaten owl, but I also know people who mix Jack Daniels with cola and refuse third helpings of woodcock. I used to brag that I'd eat anything I could spell, but you can leave out most of anything that starts with the letters OW. If I ever develop a craving for skunk, snake or meadow mice, I'll take them straight—having my meal processed first by owl holds no special charm.

Maybe it's because I'm sort of a hunter myself that the Great Horned Owl holds such fascination for me. He may be the ultimate when it comes to efficiency; I know of nothing else so strong, silent and effective. All this coupled with a blend of rare wildness and natural dignity. A Great Horned Owl perched high in a tree coldly surveying a meadow is as regal a sight as a lion staring at a herd of zebra. And when I am fortunate enough to be afield at dusk and watch the great slow wings drift him across a field, I know I'm in the presence of majesty—where every living thing below, including me, lies subservient.

If the chance permits, go out tonight and listen to the master of the woods. Imagine what he looks like there, somewhere and everywhere, in the darkness—moon-yellow eyes and cold, horned claws—the great body swaying slightly as he speaks of life and death, chats with his lady and laughs at things that only he can understand.

Know now that the year has turned around, and up in that bitter blackness are nests of eggs that will survive the worst that winter brings, then hatch, grow, hunt and come back twelve months from now to sing their eerie New Year's song.

EVASIONS, EXCUSES AND LIES

I DON'T EXPECT a standing round of applause from anyone but my immediate family, but this is the first year in longer than I care to recall that I haven't gotten my hands on a new gun for the fall season. Not that I haven't been tempted, but I have managed to resist through a combination of character, self-denial and being more or less broke.

A friend of mine who lives in Boston has a completely different outlook on things. Where I go for logic in picking up something new he cunningly goes for sentimental romance. For example, he acquired a new Labrador retriever this past January and immediately acquired a new duck gun to go with it. Having done that he now refers to the gun as "Blackie's side-by-side," thus simultaneously convincing himself of his own unselfish goodheartedness and shunting off the wrath of his wife. He recently became a father and, as he left the bar where we had toasted the joyful event, he asked my recommendation of what would make a suitable single-barrel trap gun for an eight-pound, six-ounce baby girl.

But the thrill of buying a new gun is always there whether it's for an eight-weeks-old puppy or Baby Susan—and they won't outgrow it as quickly as they do a plastic bone or a pink rattle.

Of all the reasons to get your hands on a new gun, the worst one to talk about at home is necessity, unadorned. As specious as it sounds you're better off to mumble something like "The Doc wants me to get out more often this fall but he says I need something a little lighter to carry around. He says I ought to have a little 20-gauge—add five years to my heart." Here you've taken two birds with one story: more outings, new gun. That's hard to top, but it can be done. For example, you can add one more thing—but be careful not to lose it all by being too greedy: "Doc says he doesn't want me hunting alone too much, but Vern and Jim are spending the first few days in Alabama at his uncle's quail place . . ."

Eliciting a wife's sympathy to the point where she has memorized your stock measurements, or digs into the egg money so you can work over a few coveys down South, is usually the result of script writing and acting worth an Academy Award. If some of the stories I've heard delivered to wives were set to music you'd leave the theater whistling the hit tune.

For sheer difficulty (say No. 9 on a scale of 1 to 10) the Mt. Everest of accomplishment is bringing home a new dog just after your wife has totally redecorated the house: draperies, slipcovers and carpeting. To my knowledge this has only happened once, and it was accomplished by the head of a major oil company who deposited a large sum of money in escrow with his wife's attorney to pay for damages, if any. It can also be accomplished by sheer frontal assault combined with wit and great presence of mind. For example, a Mr. Richard W. purchased a puppy at a

Ducks Unlimited dinner while in a state of tremendous conviviality. He arrived home shortly before dawn, climbed in bed with the puppy snuggled up against his chest and dropped into a deep sleep which was shortly interrupted by his wife. He opened one eye and saw her standing over him, pointing at the puppy's head on the pillow. "What's that?" she shouted. He closed the eye, smiled, and said, "Congratulate me. I've just had a German shorthair pointer."

The true gamesman tests his mettle constantly and is much to be admired by those of us less dedicated—and he has much to offer us. Jim Rikhoff, who hates hunting in tough cover, has developed an excellent variation on the old Mitchell Maneuver. (Mitchell, who was chronically unable to connect with a crossing bird, took to wearing an eyepatch and chattering about pupillary occlusion so we would always let him walk up behind the dog and take all the straightaways.)

Rikhoff would show up for a partridge hunt with his face covered with a thick white salve that closely resembled zinc oxide ointment and would talk, most embarrassed and self-consciously, about being allergic to dried leaves. It wasn't until he'd made six consecutive misses on birds in the open that we discovered that the lotion was compounded of vanilla cake frosting heavily laced with Spanish brandy. This also explained the reason why after several shoots he had to be driven home, due to reapplying the mixture with too heavy a hand at too frequent intervals.

You must remember that a too-involved ruse is easily forgotten in moments of crisis or excitement and that the simple tried-and-true variety is still the most effective. Take the "Editor's Evasion," named for a magazine man who had taken to wearing boots of different sizes. His left boot was a size 8 while the right was a 13EE. Years before he had broken his foot and had discovered while shooting skeet in a walking cast that he was able to make a much more fluid pivot on right crossing birds.

EVASIONS, EXCUSES AND LIES

Even though his foot had long since healed he continued, wisely, to bravely explain about swelling in the ankle. He managed very nicely to avoid any hard walking and could be found as often as possible taking right-hand birds with incredible consistency due to the ease of swing he had managed with his foot flopping loosely in the one huge boot. Being a penurious devil (all editors are) he'll find some excuse in the next year or so for being able to wear the big left boot to get full mileage out of the mismatched pairs. Lacking much imagination, he'll be around with some story about being bitten in the ankle by a tarpon . . . or some other such malarkey.

We see the true sportsman, then, as fully dedicated to coming out on top amid his friends and family, one who will surely find means to create golden assets out of his leaden liabilities. His shortcomings are artfully woven into the stuff of legends and his verbal skills are the basis of outdoor classics. Only the beginner will show up at camp and retire early after avoiding all chores, claiming a muscle spasm which he covers with an ice pack. He fools no one. We all know that the rubber bottle is filled with ice cubes and gin.

While the amateur arrives with a hunting coat with the game pocket sewn shut so he won't have to carry his pheasant, the gentleman shows up with a jacket with no pockets at all, claiming they've been torn off by his pointer. He not only doesn't have to carry game, he will be given his shells by other members of the party.

I know you read outdoor writing for the vast quantities of expert advice it offers. But be that as it may, the greatest expert of all is the man who obviously can't do *anything*—then the real expert will step in and insist on doing it for him.

For example, most of this piece was actually written by Ed Zern.

AFTER DARK

THE TWILIGHT FLIGHT of woodcock from the day's resting place to the nighttime feeding grounds is called "dusking." I've sort of picked up the same kind of habit—but for different reasons. My feeding tastes are not quite those of the woodcock but we seem to share certain instincts.

I like to walk away from the problems of the day come evening time and make my way back home in the growing dark. This is the soft part of the day, and the wash of oncoming night has a calming touch. There's a special comfort standing in the meadow while pheasant glide down around me to roost. The cackle of satisfaction as they find a favorite spot is about the last of the daylight sounds around here, and after a few exchanges of gossip and bragging, they settle down to sleep, pausing, no doubt, as I do, to be lulled into whatever dreams they dream by the tenor of peepers and the basso profundo of bullfrogs.

As the one world takes over from the other under starlight I am convoyed by owls impatient for me to be on my way and leave them to their sifting of the field. Silver threads are stitched by muskrats across the surface of the pond. A largemouth bass bullies his way through a school of shiners and a pair of mallards indignantly sculls away across the pond to get to the far side of me. An owl recites "Who cooks for you, who cooks for you?" as I walk the last few minutes homeward to my own supper, leaving the late diners alone outside to gather theirs.

Somehow, still reluctant to leave the dark things to their night, I stand and wait to take just one more piece of quiet with me—something that I can carry on to bed to use as an anchor against the coming of the day, soothing sound to carry in the chamber of my ear. But there is to be no sweet lullaby this night. Instead, the flinty barking of a fox chips away the softness of the moment—cold reminder, added to the owl, that there are few who ever sleep an uninterrupted sleep more than once.

BEWARE THE MAN WITH
TWENTY-THREE GUNS

I SUPPOSE THAT most of you are familiar with one or another of the newspaper columns, usually titled "Dear Something-or-Other," that deal with personal problems. Now for some reason, there has never been this type of advice offered to sportsmen. But people who hunt or fish are constantly beset with various tribulations, and I'm sure that many of the problems are common ones that, if aired and given a responsible answer, may serve to help all of us.

For example, I received a tragic telephone call the other day from a man who was clearly near the end of any hope. Several times during our conversation his voice broke and I had to murmur consoling words just to allow him time to pull himself together. Since his shattering trauma is not unusual I don't feel that I'm betraying a confidence to mention it here in some detail.

BEWARE THE MAN WITH 23 GUNS

His call was centered around the fact that he has twenty-three trap guns and none of them is exactly right. Obviously he needs help—more so since his average is about 97 despite the handicap of not having the right gun—which just goes to show what a plucky fellow he really is. Lord knows he's tried to help himself as best he can, but there's only so much a man can do before he must turn to others to help or at least ease his burden through kind and sympathetic understanding.

Although he'd begun to suspect it, he never really knew that he needed professional advice until the day his wife (who was only trying to find a way to bring him back to where he could carry on in his job and talk to his family) bought him a Purdey. He took one look at the gun, realized it had an eighth of an inch too much cast-off and took it outside to prop up a sagging screen door. His sympathetic company president was on the verge of sending him on a week of quail shooting at his private club when he realized that if our friend discovered that he didn't have the *right* quail gun the problems would reach almost unsolvable proportions.

I say, both in pride and humility, that it was from these depths that he sought my advice. I comforted him as best I could and then talked with his wife, who filled me in about the Purdey incident and the quail shoot. I was told that money was no object but time was critical, since several major state and zone shoots were coming up and they were desperately concerned that he might, heaven forfend, turn to skeet or even big-bore rifle shooting if something weren't done and done quickly.

Obviously this wasn't a problem that could be solved overnight, so I contacted a gunsmith friend of mine who owned a try-gun, and had this sent out. The therapeutic effect of fiddling with the endless adjustments of length of pull, pitch, drop at comb and heel is sometimes almost miraculous in itself, but it always provides at least a temporary elevation of spirits and in this case it

155

seemed to be working. In a week his wife called to say that he was back on the practice trap, shooting straightaways from Station Three, but wouldn't take any handicap targets and, if asked to at least try a few from his assigned 27 yards, he would merely laugh and, that night, shut himself in the cellar with his reloader.

The problem, as you have probably already seen, was to convince him of the great truth that every dedicated trapshooter instinctively knows he must some day come to grips with: *There is no perfect trapgun.* You probably also know that trapshooters cling to the dream of the perfect gun long after they have openly admitted that they do not believe in Santa Claus or the Easter Bunny, no matter how hard their wives and children try to preserve these innocent beliefs.

After a long and serious talk with him, as he fiddled with the try-gun, the truth came out. He didn't want twenty-three guns. He believed—in fact was brought up to believe—that a trapshooter only needs one gun. He quoted a lot of old sayings he'd heard as a boy, such as "Beware the man with one gun," "A man only deserves one good gun and one good dog," and the like. His fixation was deep and at first seemed unmovable. His sense of inadequacy was based on the fact that he had twenty-three guns. He had begun to question his manhood. His ability to be a decent citizen, he said, didn't require twenty-three votes.

And then it struck me. All along he had been thinking negatively and the number "twenty-three" had somehow been construed as a wretched excess when, in fact, the opposite was true. I stopped him in mid sentence and said, "You only have twenty-three trap guns?" *Only* twenty-three? He was suddenly taken aback.

"What do you mean *only?*" he asked me.

"I can think of several situations that you probably don't have a gun for," I insisted. "Do you have an over-and-under bored cylinder and light modified for shooting doubles at high-altitude gun clubs in the West?" He faltered and I quickly went on. "Do you have a single barrel bent upwards enough to center the pattern twenty-four inches above the point of aim for targets at Lordship when the onshore wind reaches a velocity of Force 5?" His face whitened. The meaning of my questions had struck deeply at the root of his problems.

"Do you know how many 200 straights have been shot in eighty years at Travers Island?" I asked him.

"Only two, I think," he answered.

"Why is that?" I said. "Because of all that nonsense about one gun or two or three. There won't be another 200 there until you—or someone just like you—sees the problems, arrives at the club with a couple of dozen guns and is fully prepared to switch from gun to gun so he can meet the problems of light and wind with intelligence and not rely on some age-old myth as an excuse."

I continued seeing that the tide had turned and he was at least beginning to listen to reason. I reminded him that at any decent-size shoot he could find a lot more than twenty-three different guns and there were indeed a lot of trap guns he didn't have. He brightened up considerably at that and said, "I don't have a Cashmore, or an Atkins or an Evans or even a Boswell." I knew then, for certain, that he had regained his true sense of proportion and that I could call his wife and tell her to stop worrying. (Trapshooters' wives start to get very nervous when a month or so passes without the husband showing up with a new gun, the way they would when a baby suddenly starts refusing food.)

He stood up to leave and started to thank me when I stopped him. "Don't thank me," I said. "My reward will be the day—and I know it will come soon—when I'm standing around watching you shoot and I overhear someone say, 'Beware the man with twenty-three guns!'"

MARTIN

HE STOOD THERE in his tired shoes and said, "I'm your guide, my name is Martin." I introduced myself and we got in my car and headed for the goose blinds. Martin's tidewater voice was rough-edged from tobacco and whiskey, and what I could see of his sun-varnished face in the glow of his cigarette seemed tired and distant.

He discussed the possibilities of geese in the same tone of voice a stockbroker might use in telling you about a stock, at once hopeful and yet restrained enough to cushion the possibilities of disappointment. To Martin this was completely serious, to me it was the beginning of a two-day lark. He was being paid to satisfy me, I was paying him to have someone to talk to and help while I hid out from the world and tried my damnedest not to think at all. I'm sure that he wouldn't remember now who I am or what I looked like—just another faceless sport in some sort of outdoor fancy dress. I was looking for a chance to do something different, to talk to strangers, to get outside myself and, if things went well, to take a pair or so of geese.

To Martin I was just another job. Another day of bitter cold, too little sleep, listening to another self-important man describe a world that Martin neither knew nor understood.

Just before the full dawn, when the geese began to work along the edge of the fields, suspicious of the decoys and the corn-husk blind, I felt a change in Martin. He wanted me to shoot—and yet he didn't. I could tell it by the way he called—part love song and part warning. Hoping that the geese would come down almost low enough to tease me into shooting so the whole skyful would turn and flare away—so it would be my fault that nothing fell, my fault that our secret place would be exposed for what it was. I let the too-high flock go on and then told Martin not to call at all unless I asked him to. I said that I'd rather wait and take my chances on some single birds that we could see aloft, I didn't take to shooting out of flocks of more than three to five. And anyway I was in no hurry to limit out and spend the whole day in the lodge.

"Tell me about yourself, Martin," I asked him. "I like the sound of your voice. I like the sound of the South in it."

"Not much to tell about, being just a guide and all, except that I help out with the fishing boats in the summer season," he offered reluctantly.

"What does a guide have to do?" I prodded.

"Well, I start early in the year before the season opens and help the other boys build these blinds. Nights I repaint and fix the decoys. We work on the boats for the water rigs, make sure the blinds don't have any beans or corn around them so we don't get brought up before the judge for baiting. And all this time I like to study all about the geese."

He stopped to see if I was at all interested in how he felt about the geese. I was. "See that old bird out there?" And he pointed to a single goose weaving serpentines above some sky-busting shooters along the sea front. "He's the old widower." I waited, watching Martin watch the single goose. "Nobody to talk to nights, nobody to take care of his things and nobody else wants him around . . . I suppose because nobody wants to see what they'll be like, come hell or high water, sooner or later. Even geese."

"He does sound a little different," I said, after we had both listened to his wail for a few minutes.

"Yessir," Martin continued, still watching the goose, "a real good goose guide likes to see them shot because they're looking and talking to geese that just ain't there, ghost geese, and that makes the others spooky."

I was just about to ask him if I ought to risk a shot if he should come down a little bit over our blind, when Martin went on. "I'm not a real good guide, sir," he said, then sat silent.

"You don't want to shoot the old fellow, Martin?" I asked him.

"No sir," he said. "I'm not a real good guide. All the good guides are off with the lodge regulars, no offense meant, sir. But it's late in the season and the birds are awful shy and I'm not the best caller in the country. I used to be pretty good but I sort of lost my lip, the way horn players do sometimes."

"Tell you what, Martin," I said. "Just for the hell of it, let's see you try and talk that old fellow down here so I can take his picture. I don't want to shoot a goose that'll be tough as a hip boot anyway."

I put my old Model 12 in the corner of the blind and started fiddling with my camera. Martin reached in his pocket and brought out another goose call that I hadn't seen before. In fact I'd never seen one like it anywhere. It was about a foot long, obviously handmade, and not made yesterday, either, by the deep, mellow, hand-polished look of it.

"This was my daddy's," Martin said. "I don't use it much any more except to fool with before gunning season, but I'll give it a little touch and we'll see what happens."

Then Martin crept out of the blind about thirty feet and, laying himself face down in the ditch, he began to sing his song; an old man's song that told of times gone by. As the shrilly mellow notes began I watched the single goose. His neck began to weave back and forth as he searched the field below for the source of the sound. His wing beats, before sort of pathetically aimless, now surged with purpose and with one swift glide he was strutting in and around our stool. After a moment he stopped and stood stark still. Martin had stopped calling, but the goose stood there and asked his question to the wooden flock. No answer came. He asked again and still there was only quiet. He cocked his head to one side and looked a moment longer, quizzically. Then, as though he had received an answer he expected, his gaze broke away.

And then, not in panic or fear, he began to run toward the open field until he began to fly, higher and higher in a tight silent spiral until he was lost from sight.

Martin came back and rejoined me on the plank seat. I suggested that we call it a day, get the bird dogs out and have a try for quail, since it didn't look like a good goose day after all.

The next morning when I looked for Martin he wasn't there, but a younger man came up to me and said that Martin had been assigned to another party. He said he would guide me and that he was sorry about Martin not being able to call geese, but he could and I'd have my limit in no time flat.

The young man was as good as his word, and by the time the working people were up having breakfast we were back at the lodge. In the car I asked the young man about Martin. "Don't rightly know, sir. He just comes in the morning and does his work and goes home at night. Seems like a nice man. But he's awful quiet. Come to think of it I never called him nothing but Martin. I don't even know if it's his first name or his last."

I suddenly realized that I didn't know if Martin was his given name or not myself. And somehow it seemed wrong for me not to know, or worse, not to have cared.

But maybe Martin didn't want to tell me. As I thought again about that morning with the single goose, the more I realized that Martin was really there with *him*—not me. And that Martin has something else to talk to when he wants to, that understands him a lot better than I could have at that time—and for a long time to come. If I'm lucky.